THE EUGENICS OF PRESIDENT ABRAHAM LINCOLN

His German and Scotch Ancestry
Irrefutably Established From
Recently Discovered Documents

by
James Caswell Coggins
A.M., S.T.D., Ph.D., LL.D.

THE CONFEDERATE
REPRINT COMPANY
☆ ☆ ☆ ☆
WWW.CONFEDERATEREPRINT.COM

The Eugenics of President Abraham Lincoln
by James Caswell Coggins

Originally Published in 1940
by Goodwill Press
Elisabethton, Tennessee

Reprint Edition © 2014
The Confederate Reprint Company
Post Office Box 2027
Toccoa, Georgia 30577
www.confederatereprint.com

Cover and Interior Design by
Magnolia Graphic Design
www.magnoliagraphicdesign.com

ISBN-13: 978-0692309506
ISBN-10: 0692309500

STARTLING STATEMENTS

"My right name is Enloe, but I have always gone by the name of my step-father." – Abraham Lincoln

"After Nancy Hanks was married to the man, Lincoln, the boy was known by the name of 'Abraham Lincoln.'" – Judge Gilmore

"It was generally understood in the community that the man that married the president's mother was not the father of the president, but that his name was Enloe." – Col. C.T. Davis

"Thomas and Nancy had one child, Sarah, and their friends after Nancy's death tried to fix the records to date back the marriage, and failed signally." – Mrs. Manon, daughter of John Hanks

ACKNOWLEDGMENT

    We wish to here express our appreciation of the valuable pioneer work by the late Hon. James H. Cathey, whose exhaustive and untiring researches resulted in producing the overwhelming evidence that Abraham Lincoln possessed a far worthier ancestry than that usually presented in popular history.

    Mr. Cathey collected the proof to substantiate his thesis forty years ago, while many of the old people were still alive and whose unimpeachable testimony we are presenting to our readers in the first few pages of this book together with the evidence which we collected, in the form of affidavits, clearly establishing the true birth-place of Abraham Lincoln in Rutherford County, North Carolina.

ILLUSTRATIONS

☆ ☆ ☆ ☆

Picture of Wesley Enloe, Lincoln's Half-Brother 37

Nancy Hank's Log Cabin Home in North Carolina 60

Nancy Hollifield, Playmate of Nancy Hanks 92

Abraham Lincoln's Mother in the Ox-Wagon 96

The True Birthplace of Abraham Lincoln North of Bostic 102

A Paul Revere Ride 106

Meeting Wild Indians 114

Tom Whipped Both Nancy and Little Abe 120

Little Abe's Father Fights Tom Lincoln 123

Picture of Scroop Enloe, Half-Brother of Lincoln 142

The Grave of Nancy Hanks, Lincoln's Mother 156

Camping at Night in the Wilderness 200

Taking Little Abraham to Kentucky. 211

Trees Used As Brakes 222

TABLE OF CONTENTS

☆ ☆ ☆ ☆

INTRODUCTION
    The Science of Eugenics and Heredity 13
    Honesty in Writing History 14

CHAPTER ONE
    A Pioneer Blazes the Trail For Future Historians 21

CHAPTER TWO
    Testimony of Philip Dills 27
    Testimony of Walker Battle 28
    Testimony of William H. Conley 29
    Testimony of Captain Ep. Everett 30
    Testimony of C. A. Ragland, Esq. 30
    Testimony of Captain James W. Terrell 31
    Testimony of Hon. Wm. A. Dills 33
    Testimony of Joseph A. Collins 34
    Testimony of H. J. Beck 36
    Testimony of D. K. Collins 36
    Testimony of Captain Wm. A. Enloe 37
    Testimony of Wesley M. Enloe 38
    Testimony of Rev. S. E. Kennedy 38
    Certificate of Professional and Business Men 41

CHAPTER THREE
    Long Slumbering Evidence of Lincoln's True Birth-Place . . 43
    Story of Brackston Smart 44
    Story of George DePriest's 45
    Story of Attorney C. O. Riding 46
    Story of J. N. Jones 48
    Story of A. De.K. Wallace 49
    Story of Edmond Dills 50
    Story of Mrs. Martha Keeter 51

Story of General Theodore Davidson 52
Story of Preston Bostic 53
Story of David Hyde of Stecoah, Graham County, N.C. . . . 54

CHAPTER FOUR
Magazine and Newspaper Endorsement 59
Strong Editorial Endorsement of N.C. Tradition 60
President Ganes Bears Testimony 64
James P. Cook's Endorsement 65
"Nancy Hanks, Her Home in North Carolina" 66

CHAPTER FIVE
A Recent Discovery 71
Two Old Manuscripts Show Lincoln's German Blood 72

CHAPTER SIX
Abraham Lincoln's Ancestry Not "White Trash" 77
Lincoln's Mother Was Not a Hanks 79
"A Remarkable Document" 81

CHAPTER SEVEN
The Great American Sphinx 83
Violence to the Basic Principles of Historical Research 85

CHAPTER EIGHT
The Enloe Family's Ancestry 89
Abraham Enloe 90

CHAPTER NINE
Nancy Hanks Enters the Enloe Home 93

CHAPTER TEN
The Enloes Move to the Mountains 97

CHAPTER ELEVEN
Nancy Hanks is Driven From Home 101

CHAPTER TWELVE
Nancy Prepares To Go To Kentucky With "Little Abe" 105
Nancy Meets Her Father 107

CHAPTER THIRTEEN
Nancy Hanks' Kentucky Beau 111
Thomas Lincoln Was Hired to Marry Nancy 113

CHAPTER FOURTEEN
The Wedding – Little Abe a Guest 117
Elizabethtown Stories 120
The Wrong Enloe in the Elizabethtown Story 121
Nancy, Tom's Wife, Receives Money 124
"Lincoln in His Shirttail" 126

CHAPTER FIFTEEN
Historical Vandalism 129
Stories of Abe's Early Childhood 131

CHAPTER SIXTEEN
"Filtering" Stories at Hodgensville 135
Abraham Lincoln Tells It 137

CHAPTER SEVENTEEN
Dr. Barton's "Cuckoo Nest" 141
The Enloe Family is Ashamed of the Scandal 142

CHAPTER EIGHTEEN
The Abbreviated Abraham Lincoln 145
Lincoln a Hunter 147
Lincoln's Moving Speech Before a Jury 150

CHAPTER NINETEEN
Lincoln Apotheosized By Historians 153
The Popular Date of Lincoln's Birth is Untenable. 155

CHAPTER TWENTY
The Death of Lincoln's Mother 159
Dr. Graham's Affidavit in Full 162
Scrutinizing the Affidavit 171
Gossip About the Cause of Nancy's Death 173

CHAPTER TWENTY-ONE
Robert Lincoln's Inherited Mental Qualities 177
A Strange Thing in Robert Lincoln's Will 179
Robert Knows the Story 180

CHAPTER TWENTY-TWO
The Evidence "Under Lock and Key" 183
The Rosetta Stone 184

CHAPTER TWENTY-THREE
Was Herndon, Lincoln's Partner, a Judas? 187
Witnesses For the Plaintiff – Herndon 189
Judge Peters' Affidavit 195
Mr. Ward Lamon 196

CHAPTER TWENTY-FOUR
Little Abraham Rides Between Thomas and Nancy 197

CHAPTER TWENTY-FIVE
Res Adjudicata – The "Fixed Date" 199

CHAPTER TWENTY-SIX
The Negro-Blood Story – A Malicious Slander 203

CHAPTER TWENTY-SEVEN
Startling Testimony 207
The Truth Comes Out 208

CHAPTER TWENTY-EIGHT
Lincoln's Letters and Nancy Hanks' Oven-Lid 211
The Old Indian Guide 212

CHAPTER TWENTY-NINE
Summation of the Evidence 217
Kentucy Stories Corroborate 218
Identification of the N.C. Girl as Lincoln's Mother 221

CHAPTER THIRTY
A Biographical Sketch of Abraham Enloe 223
Establishing a Friendship With the Cherokee Indians 229

INTRODUCTION

The Science of Eugenics and Heredity

Some years ago when I was visiting a Mr. Fletcher, a prominent and successful Dairyman of Fletcher, North Carolina, and after looking at his beautiful herd, he said; "you have not seen my best cow. Come, and I will show you a real cow." He took me around to another lot and showed me his prize cow. I was surprised to see one of the most beautiful cows in the world, almost the color of pure gold with dark trimmings around her eyes and nose. "This cow," continued Mr. Fletcher, "will give about six gallons of milk a day and will produce about three pounds of butter."

Then, when I asked about that cow's ancestry, the Dairyman replied, that there was a mystery about that cow! He had bought the cow when she was a calf from an old colored man who worked for Mr. George Vanderbilt at the Dairy barn near Asheville, N.C. And the darkie told Mr. Fletcher that Mr. Vanderbilt's finest prize Jersey, and this colored care-taker's cow brought calves the same night; and it happened to be a very dark and rainy night when the calves came, and "they, somehow, got mixed up" so the old Negro didn't know which was which."

However, this cow of "mystery" was a perfect picture of

Mr. Geo. Vanderbilt's finest registered Jersey.

Now, it will appear as the reader follows this story, that sometimes people "get mixed up" and go through life, wearing the wrong names, and among these Abraham Lincoln and his mother furnish the most outstanding examples of all history; both of these wore the wrong names through life, and it is this writer's purpose to reveal the true ancestry of Lincoln and his mother.

The Science of Eugenics and Heredity now demand for President Lincoln a far superior intellectual ancestry to the "subnormal" (Beverage) Thomas Lincoln; and the same is true of Lincoln's mother, who was far superior to the Hankses. It is now thought by psychologists that a child can not be any more intellectual than its ancestors, and if this were true the world would have never heard of Abraham Lincoln. If his sire had been the illiterate Tom Lincoln, he could never have been the President of these United States of America.

I have made a special study of this matter, and will suggest that those who are rather skeptically inclined upon this question read my book entitled *The Cellular Origin and Growth of Mentality*, in which proof of this proposition is offered.

Thinking people have always been somewhat skeptical as to the ancestry of Abraham Lincoln as given in history; and now since the development of the science of Eugenics, based upon heredity, people are still more strongly inclined to disbelieve what the historians have to say about this great man's origin.

Whatever touches the life of Lincoln, touches the hearts of millions of people, for he was "the man of the people, the man of the ages!" And these people are clamorous for every crumb of information which throws any light upon the question of his correct ancestry. And the people will never be satisfied till this man's origin, is honestly traced and told without stint or deviation from the true facts as they actually happened.

Honesty in Writing History

In a chapter devoted to "Historical Research," in his able work entitled, *The Technique of Research in Education*, Dr. C.C.

Crawford, of the Southern University of California, submits the following principles as a guide to students in the work of historical research:

>1. All research aims, or should aim, at the truth, the whole truth, and nothing but the truth.
>2. The purpose of history, as it is commonly written, is to shed light upon the present, or provide guidance for the future. This purpose causes a strong urge to introduce good moral lessons or sociably desirably conclusions from the facts rather than the conclusions which are actually true to the facts.
>
>For example it is with difficulty that the historian breaks away from the story of Washington and the Cherry Tree, because it is too dear to our hearts, and has such a splendid moral lesson.
>
>3. Next to the factor of moral influence as an enemy of historical truth is that of interest. By exaggerating or distorting the facts the history may be given a much more interesting flavor than that attached to the drab reality.
>
>A fact may be uninteresting or even of bad moral influence, but if it is really a fact, the historian has no license to omit or distort it. His object should always be to present as complete and true a picture of past events as is possible, regardless of the moral or social implications.

It may be assumed from the above quotations from Professor Crawford, that too many historians have been guilty of writing "Cherry Tree Stories" for history and expecting the people to believe everything they say; their "Old Santa Claus" still conies down the chimney, while Truth is hiding behind the door laughing up her sleeve.

We feel that we were fortunate in being able to use Dr. Crawford's able work as a text book in one of our Graduate courses, some years ago in the University of Tennessee; and while no historian, as far as I know, has put into practice all the valuable rules and suggestions offered, it is our purpose to follow them as closely as it is possible, and give the people the real truth instead of a nice "Cherry Tree Story."

It has often been contended, that Abraham Lincoln furnished a good example of the doctrine of evolution, as something great coming from almost nothing, and this case is the favorite proof text for this popular theory. But one does not need a high brow to be able to see the sophistry lying at the foundation of all such foolishness. The word "evolve, evolution," comes from the Latin *"e"* meaning out of and *"volo; volere"* to turn, and hence the meaning, to turn out, or pour out a thing, or to unroll something. But one can see the utter impossibility of "pouring out" a bucket of water, if there is no water in the bucket to start with. And if the bucket is full of milk it is impossible to pour out water. Now this gets right at the foundation of that whole high-sounding question, and any school boy or school girl can, in a few words, furnish an unanswerable puzzle to such teachers.

It has been proved, over and over again, that something can not come from nothing; and that any kind of egg must "evolute" the same kind of life, bird or animal, that produced the egg. It does not switch off to something different. The seed of the African Race can only produce Negroes; the seed of the Chinese can only produce the Chinese, and it takes the seed of the White Race to produce White People. This is an unchangeable law. Not only is this a fixed law as applied to the different Races of people, but this is also true of families, and of different individuals. Compare the "Jukes Family" of New York with the family of Robert E. Lee, or George Washington, and see how "evolution" works. The truth is as proved, that its slant is downward instead of upward.

And the scientists have now arrived at the conclusion, that it is utterly impossible for people of sub-normal intellect to produce offspring of intellect above the average. In fact they are unable to produce offspring superior in mind to themselves.

Then, one can see that it would have been utterly impossible for Abraham Lincoln, of splendid intellect, far above the average, to have been the offspring of Tom Lincoln, who was below the average, and, by Senator Beverage, is called a "sub-normal in mind." This old illiterate liquor-maker, not far superior to "the Jukes" was not the father of Abraham Lincoln; and a man of normal mentality could not have been "hired" to marry a woman and rear her child, already born.

In releasing the matter contained in this book, this writer has simply collected and correlated the pertinent and outstanding facts, so long stumbled over by writers unsympathetic with this viewpoint, the large majority preferring to join the "Spade" Brigade (William E. Barton) in flagrant violation of the first fundamental principle laid down by Dr. Crawford, to be observed in all historical research.

And we feel constrained, in simple justice, to say, had it not been for the very earnest request of prominent citizens of Western North Carolina, about Asheville, among whom were the late Dr. Foster A. Sondley, LL.D., the Hon. Lock Craig, a former Governor of North Carolina, Judge Henry B. Stephens, and the Rev. Baxter S. Tipton, a staunch Republican and great admirer of Abraham Lincoln, never would we have written a word upon this subject; and the reason for this will be detected by the careful reader.

Now the work is done, and I send this book forth with the hope that it may clear up the great "Lincoln mystery" by furnishing a back-ground commensurate with Lincoln's greatness.

– the Author

CHAPTER ONE

A Pioneer Blazes The Trail For Future Historians

The following is Hon. J.H. Cathey's foreword to his first book (1899):

Generous reader, traverse with me the ensuing pages and they shall open to you a "sealed book." They shall lead along the neglected path of unwritten history and reveal to you, with care, an interesting fact in the story of America's most remarkable man.

They may tear the veil of popular modesty only to discover the naked truth.

The truth cannot hurt the living or the dead.

It is often a good popular nervine to disturb the commonplace with the heroic, the romantic, the tragic.

It is better still to replace popular shadow of doubt with popular sunshine of fidelity.

It is said: "There is a skeleton in every closet and that must not be disturbed." There is no avoiding it with individuals or aggregations.

There should be no attempt to avoid exploring the dimmest recesses in the life of a real hero. The life and acts of a real hero are not circumscribed by narrow lines. The atmosphere that belongs to him at once becomes free and self-imparting. Each and every phase of him is of the intensest interest to humanity; at once becomes, and of right should become, a common heritage.

Tradition is the musty old closet in which has been stowed for thousands of years the disjointed skeletons of history. These should be haled forth, articulated, clothed with the flesh, and animated with the blood of the living truth.

There is one narrative of human events in which there is no evidence of a traditional closet – the Bible. In this ancient bundle of truth "a spade is called a spade."

If the "man after God's own heart" took his fellow's life that he might obtain his wife, this book says so in so many blunt words. If the "father of the faithful" drove his bond-woman and their illegitimate son into the wilderness to die to please his irate wife, such is the record.

But it is not our purpose here to try to reconcile moral incongruities. It should be sufficient for one to reflect that our world is inhabited by men; that it has been so and doubtless will.

Yielding to a moral cowardice, a feeling that recoils at the thought of making public one's own faults, historians have, with a few refreshing exceptions, cast aside one-half the events of the world.

The custom to pass unnoticed the vices, which make up the larger moiety of the man, has led them to an immoderate exaggeration of his virtues.

To these, and a false notion of taste, is traceable the failure to record volumes without number of the most thrilling history. Here is the trysting place of truant tradition and family lore. Here, too, is a faithful nursery of individual and national hypocrisy.

The recording of the good only, in the life of a person or a nation, is a tale half told, a song half sung – often a wondrous tale, an epic song.

The statue is not complete until the sculptor has watched the last-minute characteristic of the original follow the errand of his chisel. The flower does not show forth all its delicate tints in rounded splendor till its last tender petal is full blown.

THE EUGENICS OF ABRAHAM LINCOLN

Cicero tells us that the first and fundamental law of history is, "That it should neither dare to say anything that is false or fear to say anything that is true, nor give any just suspicion of favor or disaffection."

This is the standard of the true historian. Apropos to this, Edward Evert Hale says, "The history of mankind is made up of the biographies of men." If this be true, Cicero's standard will apply to biography with double force.

The scriptural narrative traces the lineage of Christ along a solid chain of forty-two generations. If the sacred chronicler essayed to trace, without trepidation, so remote an origin as that of the divine Christ, why should one tremble or hesitate to inquire after the beginning of a great, though finite man? The day of miracles is past these eighteen hundred years, and something cannot come of nothing.

It is the historical teaching that Abraham Lincoln was virtually "without ancestors, fellows, or successors." Whether this is a delusion it does not concern us to argue. He came into the world and the world understood him not.

It is, therefore, the sole purpose of this little book [*Truth is Stranger Than Fiction*] to present a tradition tending to prove that this wonderful man was not without ancestors. His mother was Nancy Hanks. If he was the son of a worthy sire the world is entitled to know who that sire was; when, where and how he lived; whence he came and what his characteristics.

For ninety years [about forty years ago this book was written], or thereabout, from the time it is said Abraham Lincoln was begotten or born, as the case was, and the breeze occurred in the Enloe home, there has subsisted among the honest people at the center of authority a lively tradition that Abraham, the head of the Enloe family, was Lincoln's father by Nancy Hanks, who occupied the position of servant-girl in the Enloe household.

So confident and persistent have the keepers of this old testimony to the origin of Lincoln been, when plied with interrogatories, that they knew what they were talking about, that there was no opening for superstition, and the most one who was inclined to be skeptical could do, was to wonder and say nothing.

One might hug his incredulity by imagining that the people who fathered the strange accounts of Nancy Hanks and Abraham Enloe and a child, and the wonderful story of the striking personal likeness of Abraham Lincoln and Wesley Enloe, are illiterate, fanatical folk who have conjured up a fragmentary fable, how and for what they know not; but this incredulity is all cleared away, like fog before the sunbeams, when one learns that the custodians of the "Lincoln Tradition" are numbered by the scores and hundreds of the people, men and women, of Western North Carolina.

Ladies as well as gentlemen, not only of the immediate section, but also of distant States, visiting at Asheville and other places of resort in our mountains, finding a thread of the tradition, they pulled until their curiosity, at last becoming excited, they visited Wesley Enloe, the alleged half-brother of Abraham Lincoln, in his hospitable mountain home, were filled with amazement, and went away convinced that the tradition was made of cords that could not easily be broken.

People who were familiar with Mr. Lincoln's history, or who knew him personally, were struck with the strange physical resemblance on first sight, and then watched a series of impersonations of Lincoln as they studied the features and noted the varying postures of Wesley Enloe.

The remarkable tradition, with its flesh and blood corroboration, was from time to time engaged to be written up by journalists, lawyers and clergymen of culture and standing, but nothing more than a hasty, desultory newspaper article was the result. The people over a very limited area of population were being made conversant with the valuable tradition and its worthy repositors were, one by one, stepping from the earthly stage. It was plainly apparent that in a very few years the old generation would be gone, and a truth of American history, by sheer neglect, would be forever lost.

We felt our incapacity to undertake so responsible a task. We were conscious of the delicacy of the undertaking, but the implicit, unquestioning faith which we had in the truthfulness of the tradition gave us a courage which shrank not from the most formidable hobgoblin.

Thus emboldened we set to work to gather the odds and ends of our folk-history. We resolved at the outset that we would interrogate none but the most trustworthy people who were in the best position to give a reason for the faith that was in them, together with the story of the relatives of the distinguished subject of our memoir. This we have, in every instance, done. In 1895 the writer conceived the idea of writing a newspaper or magazine article for the simple purpose of making known the tradition to the public generally, hoping thereby to attract the attention of the enterprising journalist, and after that the enduring chronicler; but private concerns interfered, and our purpose was frustrated for the time. Luckily, however, we then obtained the statements of some very aged gentlemen whose testimony will herein appear, and which is of the most important character, who have since died.

We have been extremely fortunate in enlisting the cooperation of various good and often very distinguished citizens in our search for data. Some of these have passed away since we began our first investigation. Those who are "up and able to be about" are the venerable half-brother of our illustrious subject, Mr. Wesley M. Enloe, and his nephew, Capt. W. A. Enloe; Dr. Isaac N. Enloe, of Illinois, and Mr. Sam G. Enloe, of Missouri; Mr. J. Frank Enloe of North Carolina; and Mrs. Floyd of Texas, son and niece of Wesley M. Enloe; Mr. H.J. Beck, of Ocona Lufta, North Carolina; C. A. Ragland, Esq., of Stockton, Mo.; Mr. Joseph A. Collins, of Clyde, N.C.; Capt. E. Everett, and Mr. D.K. Collins, of Bryson City, N.C.; the venerable Philip Dills, Hon. William A. Dills, and Mr. Sion T. Early, of Dillsboro, N.C; and Capt. W. Terrell of Webster, N.C.

To each of these gentlemen, and to Mrs. Floyd, the writer wishes to express his most sincere thanks. He has been most deeply touched by the generous and always courteous response his appeals have met with from each and all of them, and his obligation to them can only be enhanced by the increase of the importance of the historical truth as it goes into the world fresh from their honest and disinterested lips. In voicing the memory of hundreds, these several individuals will, for the first time, bring face to face with the world a fact that is worth the world's while.

Tradition once said, "Premature pangs seized the mother of Napoleon while she was at church. She hurried home, barely reaching her apartment when the heroic babe was delivered, without accoucheur, on a piece of tapestry inwrought with an effigy of Achilles." Gradually becoming credulous, history says now, "This probably occurred."

There is not current a tradition of the Corsican that is entitled to more credit than the North Carolina tradition of the immortal Rail-splitter. We therefore give it to you and the future historian, as you have it, in modest but faithful form.

James H. Cathey
Bryson City, N.C.
Feb. 18, 1899

CHAPTER TWO

Testimony of Philip Dills

Mr. Dills was born in Rutherford County, N.C, January 10, 1808. His father emigrated to the mountains of Western North Carolina almost contemporaneously with Abraham Enloe. Although Mr. Dills was four years old when Jackson whipped Packenham at New Orleans, he is nimble both in body and mind. He describes the removal of the Cherokees west of the Mississippi; tells of the election when Clay and Jackson were rivals, of casting his first vote for the latter; recalls the personal appearance of John C. Calhoun, whom he saw and with whom he talked; the duel between Sam Carson and Dr. Vance, and many other incidents of early days he distinctly remembers and recites with genuine gusto.

Mr. Dills is a citizen of Jackson County. His post-office is Dillsboro. He said, "Although a generation younger and living some twenty-five miles from him, I knew Abraham Enloe personally and intimately. I lived on the road which he frequently traveled in his trips south, and he made my house a stopping place. He was a large man, tall, with dark complexion, and coarse, black hair. He was a splendid looking man, and a man of fine sense. His judgment was taken as a guide, and he was respected and looked up to in his time, "I do not know when I first heard of his relation with Nancy Hanks, but it was many years before the civil war, and while I was a very young man. The circumstance was related in my hearing, by the generation older than myself, and I heard it talked over time and again later. I have no doubt that Abraham Enloe was the father of Abraham Lincoln."

Testimony of Walker Battle

Mr. Battle was born February 12, 1809, in Haywood County. His father was one of the three men who came to Ocona Lufta with Abraham Enloe. He was a highly respected citizen of Swain County. The following statement was received from him in 1895. He has since died. His son, Milton Battle, a reputable citizen, is familiar with his father's statement. His post-office is Bryson City, N.C. Walker Battle said:

> My father was one of the first settlers of this country. He came here with Abraham Enloe. I have lived here my entire life, and I knew Abraham Enloe and his family almost as well as I knew my own.
> The incident occurred, of course, before my day, but I distinctly remember hearing my own family tell of the trouble between Abraham Enloe and Nancy Hanks when I was a boy. I recall, as if it were but yesterday, hearing them speak of Nancy's removal to Kentucky and that she married there a fellow by the name of Lincoln; that Abraham Enloe had some kind of correspondence with the woman after he sent her to Kentucky, sent her something, and that he had to be very cautious to keep his wife from finding it out.
> There is no doubt as to Nancy Hanks having once lived in the family of Abe Enloe, and there is no doubt that she was the mother of a child by him.
> No, I never saw Nancy Hanks's name in print in my life, and never saw a sketch of Abraham Lincoln, or heard of him, until he became a candidate for the presidency in 1860.

Testimony of William H. Conley

Mr. Conley was born about the year 1812, in Haywood County. He lived the greater part of his life within fifteen miles of Abraham Enloe. He was a man of intelligence and perfect veracity. The following statement, the original of which is in the writer's possession, was obtained from him in 1895. He has since died.

Mr. Conley said:

My father, James Conley, was the first white man to settle on the creek in this (Swain) county, which bears his name. Abraham Enloe was one of the first to settle on Ocona Lufta. Enloe and my father were warm friends; I knew Abe Enloe well myself. He was an impressive looking man. On first sight you were compelled to think that there was something extraordinary in him, and when you became acquainted with him your first impression was confirmed. He was far above the average man in mind.

As to the tradition: I remember when I was a lad, on one occasion some of the women of the settlement were at my father's house, and in conversation with my mother they had a great deal to say about some trouble that had once occurred between Abe Enloe and a girl they called Nancy Hanks, who had at one time stayed at Enloe's. I heard nothing more, as I now remember, about the matter, until the year before the war, the news came that Abraham Lincoln had been nominated for the presidency, when it was the common understanding among the older people that Lincoln was the son of Abe Enloe by Nancy Hanks.

Not one of them had ever seen, up to that time, a written account of Lincoln. There is no doubt that Nancy Hanks lived at Abraham Enloe's. She became pregnant there by Abraham Enloe, and to quell a family disturbance, Enloe had her moved to Kentucky, just as my father and mother have, time and again, related in my hearing.

I have no doubt that Abraham Enloe was the father of Abraham Lincoln.

Testimony of Captain Ep. Everett

Captain Everett was born on April 4, 1830, in Davy Crockett's native county, Tennessee. He came to what was then Jackson, now Swain, County in the late fifties, and has since lived in twelve miles of the Abe Enloe homestead. He was Captain of Company & Third Tennessee. He served through the entire war, showing conspicuous courage at First Manassas. He helped to organize the County of Swain, in 1871. He was a member of the constitutional convention of 1875, which amended the constitution of the State. He has been Magistrate, Mayor of the town of Bryson City, and Sheriff of the county. He is well known throughout the State as one of the best and most brainy citizens.

He said:

> In time of the war, in conversation with old and reliable citizens of this section, I learned that Abe Lincoln's mother, Nancy Hanks, once lived in the family of Abe Enloe and was sent from there to Kentucky to be delivered of a child. The cause of her removal to Kentucky was a threatened row between Abe Enloe and old Mrs. Enloe, his wife. The people in this county, all the old people with whom I talked, were familiar with the girl as Nancy Hanks. This subject was not only the common country rumor, but I saw it similarly rehearsed in the local newspapers of the time. I have no doubt of its truth.

Testimony of C. A. Ragland, Esq.

C. A. Ragland, leading attorney of the town of Stockton, Mo., wrote:

> In reply, I have to say: About twelve years ago I called on Col. T. G. Davis at St. Louis, Mo. Col. Davis was a relative, his mother having been a Miss Ragland of Kentucky. Col. Davis was born in Kentucky and was a cousin of Jeff Davis, President of the Confederacy. He said he was intimately acquainted with Abraham Lincoln; was associated with him in law cases. He said he knew Lincoln's mother, was raised in that community, and it was the

general understanding that Lincoln, the man that married the president's mother was not the father of the president, but that his father's name was Enloe.

Testimony of Captain James W. Terrell

Captain Terrell was born in Rutherford County, North Carolina, the last day of the year 1829. At the age of sixteen he came to Haywood County, where he lived with his grandfather, Wm. D. Kirkpatrick, until 1852, when he joined himself in business with Col. Wm. H. Thomas, a man of great shrewdness and enterprise. In 1854 he was made disbursing agent to the North Carolina Cherokees. In 1862 he enlisted in the Confederate service as lieutenant in a company of Cherokee Indians. Later he was promoted. Since the war he has merchandised, and been a railroad contractor. He has represented his county in the legislature and filled other offices of trust and honor. He is recognized throughout Western North Carolina as a most excellent and useful citizen. He said:

> Having personally had some hints from the Enloes, of Jackson and Swain, with whom I am intimately acquainted, my attention was seriously drawn to the subject by an article which appeared in *Bledsoe's Review*, in which the writer gives an account of a difficulty between Mr. Lincoln's reputed father and a man named Enloe,
>
> I then began to inquire into the matter and had no difficulty in arriving at the following indisputable facts, for which I am indebted to the following old people: the late Dr. John Mingus, son-in-law to Abraham Enloe; his widow, Mrs. Polly Mingus, daughter of Abraham Enloe (lately deceased); and their son Abram Mingus, who still lives; also to the late William Farley and the late Hon. William Thomas, besides many other very old people, all of whom, I believe, are now dead.
>
> 1st: Some time about the beginning of the present century, a young orphan girl was employed in the family of Abraham Enloe, then of Rutherford County, North Carolina. Her position in the family was nearly that of member, she being an orphan with

no relatives that she knew. Her name was undoubtedly Nancy Hanks. Abraham Enloe moved about the year 1805 from Rutherford, stopping first for a short while on Soco Creek, but eventually settled on the Ocona Lufta, where his son, Wesley M. Enloe, now resides, then Buncombe afterward Haywood, later Jackson, and now Swain County.

2nd: Some time after settling on the Ocona Lufta, Miss Hanks became enceinte, and a family breeze resulted and Nancy Hanks was sent to Kentucky.

3rd. She was accompanied to Kentucky by or through the instrumentality of Hon. Felix Walker, then a member of Congress from the "Buncombe District."

There is no doubt of the truth of these statements. They were all of them well known to a generation just passed away, and with many of whom I was well and intimately acquainted. The following I give as it came to me.

A probable reason for sending the girl, Nancy Hanks, to Kentucky, was that at that time some of the Enloe kindred were living there. I was informed that a report reached here that she was married soon after reaching Kentucky.

Mrs. Enloe's maiden name was Egerton, and she was a native of Rutherford County. Some years ago, meeting with Dr. Egerton of Hendersonville, and finding that he was a relative of Mrs. Enloe, our conversation drifted toward the Enloe family, and he imparted to me the following:

Some time in the early fifties two young men of Rutherford County moved to Illinois and settled near Springfield. One of them, whose name was Davis, became intimately acquainted with Mr. Lincoln. In the fall of 1860, just before the presidential election, Mr. Davis and his friend paid a visit back to Rutherford and spent a night with Dr. Egerton. Of course the presidential candidates would be discussed. Mr. Davis told Dr. Egerton that in a private and confidential talk which he had with Mr. Lincoln the latter told him that he was of Southern extraction, that his right name was, or ought to have been, Enloe, but that he had always gone by the name of his stepfather.

Mr. Enloe's Christian name was Abram, and if Mr. Lincoln was his son he was not unlikely named for him.

About the time of the famous contest between Lincoln

and Stephen A. Douglas, Hon. W. H. Seward franked to me a speech of Mr. Lincoln's, made in that campaign, entitled: "Speech of Hon. Abram Lincoln." He himself invariably signed his name "A. Lincoln."

To my mind, taking into consideration the unquestioned fact that Nancy Hanks was an inmate of Abraham Enloe's family, that while there she became pregnant, that she went to Kentucky and there married an obscure man named Lincoln, the story is highly probable indeed, and when fortified with the wonderful likeness between Wesley M. Enloe and Mr. Lincoln, I cannot resist the conviction that they are sons of the same sire. A photo of either might be passed on the family of the other as their genuine head.

Testimony of Hon. Wm. A. Dills

Mr. Dills is a native of Jackson County, N.C, and resides in the thriving little town which was named in his honor, Dillsboro. His people have honored him with place and power. He has represented his county in the lower house of the legislature. He said:

My information is traditional, as the events named occurred long before I was born.

Several years ago, while I was teaching a school in the State of Missouri, I read a sketch of the life of Abraham Lincoln, which ran as follows:

"Abraham Lincoln was born in the State of Kentucky, of a woman whose name was Nancy Savage or Nancy Hanks. His father is supposed to have been a man by the name of Enloe. When the boy was eight years old his mother married an old man by the name of Lincoln, whose profession was rail-splitting. Soon after the marriage he took a large contract of splitting rails in the State of Illinois, where he took the boy and his mother, and the boy assumed the name of Lincoln." The above is a verbatim quotation of the sketch that far.

On my return from Missouri I took occasion to investigate the old tradition to my own satisfaction. I found that Nancy Hanks once lived with Abraham Enloe, in the County of Buncombe (now Swain), and while there became involved with Enloe, a child was imminent, if it had not been born, and Nancy Hanks was conveyed to Kentucky.

The public may read in Wesley M. Enloe, son of Abraham Enloe, a walking epistle of Abraham Lincoln. If there is any reliance to be placed in tradition of the strongest class they are half-brothers. I have not the shadow of a doubt the tradition is true.

For further information, I refer you to Col. Allen T. Davidson, of Asheville.

Testimony of Joseph A. Collins

Mr. Collins is fifty-six years of age and resides in the town of Clyde, in Haywood County. He served three years of the war between the States as a private, after which he was promoted to the second lieutenancy of his company in which capacity he continued until the surrender. He has been in the mercantile business for twenty-five years, ten of which he was a traveling salesman. He is now proprietor of a hardware store in his home town. He is well known over the entire Western part of the State as a gentleman of the most unquestionable integrity. He said:

The first I knew of any tradition being connected with Abraham Lincoln's origin on his father's side was in 1867. At that time I was in Texas and while there I made the acquaintance of Judge Gilmore, an old gentleman who lived three miles from Ft. Worth.

He told me he knew Nancy Hanks before she was married, and that she then had a child she called Abraham. "While the child was yet small," said Judge Gilmore, "she married a man by the name of Lincoln, a whiskey distiller." "Lincoln," said Gilmore, "was a very poor man and they lived in a small log house."

"After Nancy Hanks was married to the man Lincoln," said Gilmore, "the boy was known by the name of Abraham Lincoln." He said that Abraham's mother, when the boy was about eight years old, died.

Judge Gilmore said he himself was five or six years older than Abraham Lincoln; that he knew him well; attended the same school with him. He said Lincoln was a bright boy and learned very rapidly; was the best boy to work he had ever known.

He said he knew Lincoln until he was almost grown, when he, Gilmore, moved to Texas. During his residence in Texas he was elected as Judge of the county Court. He was an intelligent, responsible man.

Years ago I was traveling for a house in Knoxville. On Turkey creek, in Buncombe County, N.C, I met an old gentleman whose name was Phillis Wells. He told me that he knew Abraham Lincoln was the son of Abraham Enloe, who lived on Ocona Lufta.

Wells said he was then ninety years of age. When he was a young man he traveled over the country and sold tin ware and bought furs, feathers, and ginsing for William Johnson, of Waynesville. He said he often stopped with Abraham Enloe. On one occasion he called to stay over night, as was his custom, when Abraham Enloe came up and went with him to the barn to put up his horse, and while there Enloe said:

"My wife is mad; about to tear up the place; she has not spoken to me in two weeks, and I wanted to tell you about it before you went in the house." Then, Wells remarked, I said "What is the matter?" and Abraham Enloe replied: "The trouble is about Nancy Hanks, a hired girl we have living with us." Wells said he stayed all that night, and that Mrs. Enloe did not speak to her husband while he was there. He said he saw Nancy Hanks there, that she was a good-looking girl, and seemed to be smart for business.

Wells said before he got back there on his next trip that Abraham Enloe had sent Nancy Hanks to Jonathan's creek and hired a family there to take care of her; that later a child was born to Nancy Hanks, and she named him Abraham.

Meantime the trouble in Abraham Enloe's family had not abated. As soon as Nancy Hanks was able to travel, Abraham Enloe hired a man to take her and her child out of the country, in order to restore quiet and peace at home. He said he sent her to some of his relatives near the State line between Tennessee and Kentucky. He said Nancy and the child were cared for by Enloe's relatives until she married a fellow by the name of Lincoln.

I asked the old gentleman if he really believed Abraham Lincoln was the son of Abraham Enloe, and he replied: "I know it, and if I did not know it I would not tell it."

I made special inquiry about the character of Wells, and every one said he was an honest and truthful man and a good citizen.

Testimony of H. J. Beck

Mr. Beck was born and reared and has all his life lived on Ocona Lufta. He was one of Abraham Enloe's neighbors, as was his father before him. He is now an octogenarian. He is well-to-do, and of an intelligent and upright character He said:

I have heard my father and mother often speak of the episode of Abraham Enloe and Nancy Hanks. They said Abraham Enloe moved from Rutherford County here, bringing with his family a hired girl named Nancy Hanks. Some time after they settled here Nancy Hanks was found to be with child, and Enloe procured Hon. Felix Walker to take her away. Walker was gone two or three weeks. If he told where he took her I do not now think of the place.

As to Abraham Enloe, he was a very large man, weighing between two and three hundred. He was Justice of the Peace. The first I remember of him, I was before him in trials. In these cases, of differences between neighbors, he was always for peace and compromise. If an amicable adjustment could not be effected, he was firm and unyielding. He was an excellent business man.

Testimony of D. K. Collins

Mr. Collins was born October 8, 1844. He was a lieutenant of Sharpshooters, company F, 69th N.C. regiment. He is the most extensive dry-goods merchant in the State west of Asheville. He is an excellent citizen and a cultured gentleman. He said: "The tradition is well-founded. I have been in position to note its bearings, and there is no doubt that Nancy Hanks lived at Abraham

Enloe's, and that the event took place substantially as related by the men and women who were familiar with it."

Testimony of Captain Wm. A. Enloe

Captain Enloe was born in Haywood (now Jackson) County and is sixty-six years of age. He is a successful merchant and business man. He is a gentleman of superior sense, modesty, firmness, and integrity. He was Captain of Company F, 29th N.C. Regiment, commanded by Robert B. Vance, and served through the war. He has represented his county in the legislature. He is a grandson of Abraham Enloe. He said:

> There is a tradition come down through the family that Nancy Hanks, the mother of President Lincoln, once lived at my grandfather's, and while there became the mother of a child said to be my grandfather's, Abraham Enloe.
> One Mr. Thompson married my aunt Nancy, daughter of Abraham Enloe, contrary to the will of my grandfather; to conceal the matter from my grandfather's knowledge, Thompson stole her away and went to Kentucky; on the trip they were married. Hearing of their marriage, my grandfather reflected and decided to invite them back home. On their return they were informed of the tumult in my grandfather's household because of Nancy Hanks, who had given birth to a child; and when my uncle and aunt, Thompson and wife, returned to their Kentucky home, they took with them Nancy Hanks and her child. This is the family story as near as I can reproduce it from memory:
> In 1861, I came home from Raleigh to recruit my company. On my return, while waiting for the stage in Asheville, I took dinner at what was then the Carolina House. The table was filled largely with officers going to and from their various commands. The topic of conversation seemed to be Abraham Lincoln.
> One of the gentlemen remarked that Lincoln was not the correct name of the President, that his name was Enloe and that his father lived in Western North Carolina. I maintained the part of an interested listener, and no one suspected my name was Enloe.

After this, during the war, and while stationed in East Tennessee I was handed a paper with nearly a column of what purported to be a sketch of Abraham Lincoln's early life in Kentucky, alleging that his father's name was Enloe, and that he, Lincoln, was born in Western North Carolina.

Testimony of Wesley M. Enloe

Mr. Enloe was born in 1811, in Haywood County, N.C, and is the ninth and only surviving son of Abraham Enloe. He resides on the same farm and in the same house where his father lived when Nancy Hanks was banished from the household. He is a quiet, suave, intelligent gentleman of the old school, and a prosperous farmer. He said:

> I was born after the incident between my father and Nancy Hanks. I have, however, a most vivid recollection of hearing the name Nancy Hanks frequently mentioned in the family while I was a boy.
> No, I never heard my father mention it. He was always silent on the subject as far as I know.
> Nancy Hanks lived in my father's family. I have no doubt the cause of my father's sending her to Kentucky is the one generally alleged. The occurrence as understood by my generation, and given to them by that of my father, I have not a doubt is essentially true.
> My father moved to this place (Ocona Lufta) somewhere from 1803 to 1808.

Testimony of Rev. S.E. Kennedy

Here is the testimony of Rev. S.E. Kennedy, former minister of the Christian Church of Davis, Indian Territory (now Oklahoma): The Davis *Weekly News*, of his home town, says of him: "Rev. S.E. Kennedy is the pastor of the Christian Church here, and is loved and esteemed universally by all who have the pleasure of knowing him."

He wrote:

Picture of Wesley Enloe,
Lincoln's Half-Brother

Here we present a picture of Wesley Enloe, son of Abraham Enloe, and half-brother of Abraham Lincoln. He was the youngest of nine sons, all lived to be grown men. He was considerably over six feet high.

My grandfather and grandmother, John and Fanny Kennedy, lived neighbor to Abraham Enloe in North Carolina, and were well acquainted with both Abraham Enloe and Nancy Hanks. My grandmother was born about 1775. Her story of the Enloe-Hanks embroglio was substantially as follows:

The father (uncle) of Nancy Hanks was a drunkard and was so cruel to his wife and children that he was imprisoned and made to make shoes as a punishment. The mother of Nancy Hanks was forced, because of her inability to support them, to bind her children out. Abraham Enloe took Nancy and a man by the name of Pratt took Mandy.

Mr. and Mrs. Pratt were kind to Mandy, and taught her to card and spin and weave. Mandy did well and married Samuel Henson and moved across the mountains.

Abraham Enloe became entangled with Nancy and caused her to be taken to Kentucky and to be married to Tom Lincoln, who kept a still-house there. Abraham Enloe promised to give Tom Lincoln five hundred dollars, a wagon and pair of mules if he would marry Nancy Hanks, but after Lincoln got drunk and attempted to kill Abraham Enloe, they compromised, and Enloe gave Lincoln a mule, a mare and fifteen dollars in money whereupon Lincoln took Nancy and little Abe back to Kentucky, and I never saw them more (Cathey, pp. 39-63).

Mr. Kennedy says:

My grandmother lived to be near ninety, dying about the year 1866. She could neither read nor write, but possessed the most perfect memory I have ever observed. She knew Abraham Enloe before and after they moved across the mountains. Whether my grandparents came with Enloe when he migrated to North Carolina, I do not know. What was meant by "across the mountains" I have forgotten, if I ever knew." ("Across the mountains" was over the "Blue Ridge" from Rutherford County into the mountain country where Enloe settled.)

The foregoing overwhelming and indisputable evidence submitted by Hon. James H. Cathey deserves serious consideration. Mr. Cathey had no axe to grind in this matter as he was related in no way to the Enloes, and was a Republican and an ardent admirer of Mr. Lincoln.

Having taught school right in the heart of the community that has been for over a hundred years the center of this tradition, he, like myself, became so fully convinced of the absolute truth of this matter that he felt it his duty to preserve it for posterity.

Mr. Cathey deserves great credit for doing this important pioneer work. In this case, while he failed to locate the exact birthplace of Lincoln, he does not fail to establish the fact that Abraham Lincoln was the son of Abraham Enloe of Western North Carolina. His evidence is unanswerable. Had Mr. Cathey gone to Rutherford County in search for material, he would have located the birthplace of Abraham Lincoln, just as I have done, in the evidence which is to follow.

Certificate of Professional and Business Men

This certifies that, for many years, we, the undersigned have heard the older people relate the current story, that "Nancy Hanks, the mother of President Lincoln, was reared in Rutherford County"; and also that Lincoln was born here.

(Signed) M. L. Edwards, Attorney
R. S. Eaves, Attorney (Judge)
D. F. Morrow, Author
R. E. Price, Editor, *The News*
C. L. Miller, Banker
J. Y. Yelton, Clerk Superior Court
J. F. Flack, Clerk City Court
C. T. Waldrop, Hardware Merchant
W. A. Thompson, M. D. Physician
Jno. P. Bean, Recorder
W. C. Harden, Sheriff
W. C. Greer, Register of Deeds
J. L. Taylor, Vice-Pres. Citizen Bank
C. F. Gold, M. D., Physician
F. W. Logan, M. D., Physician

NOTE: The foregoing sworn testimonies were provided by Hon. James H. Cathey, *The Truth is Stranger Than Fiction.*

CHAPTER THREE

Long-Slumbering Evidence of Lincoln's True Birth-Place

After the lapse of many years since my mother's old uncle, Mr. B.H. Melton, had related his strange, tragic story in regard to Nancy Hanks, and the birth of her child in Rutherford County, North Carolina, I went to this place and made a very careful examination. I was perfectly astonished at the amount of reliable testimony to be yet found among the old people living there. Their tradition is absolutely unanswerable by any of the apologists.

At first this was a kind of "community secret" which the people felt they could not afford to talk about with any apparent degree of relish or approbation, as will be illustrated in the following incident:

At an election held in Rutherford County, when a man by the name of Benjamine Lovelace expressed his intention to vote for Abraham Lincoln for President, the crowd grew angry and some said "kill him," and others said "hang him." And a man by the name of Amos Harrell said, "Just let me to him." Whereupon the crowd parted for Harrell, and he ran up and kicked Lovelace out of the crowd; and Lovelace had to flee to the nearby bushes and woods and hide himself to save his life! A man by the name of Tim Haney was hanged in this same community for a trivial "political offense." The people who related these stories to me are of the very best people and were full-fledged "Democrats." So, what they told was a reflection upon their own political party, and hence they could not have been prejudiced or lying about it.

This occurred near the very spot where Abraham Lincoln was born, and the people back at this election called him a "bastard," and said they knew it was true; and his few friends could make no defense (Preston Bostic, and Mrs. Martha Keeter).

Story By Brackston Smart

Mr. Brackston Smart lives on the highway between Forest City and Ellenboro. He is a great grandson of "grannie" (Nancy) Hollifield, and owns the same farm and lives in the same house, though repaired, that was occupied by this playmate of Abraham Lincoln's mother. This is an intelligent and reputable citizen and a Baptist minister, whose place was said to be worth forty thousand dollars. His wife is a school teacher. He gave me the following information:

This old lady, his grandmother, lived to be almost a hundred and seven years old (1794-1900). During her girlhood days she was very intimately associated with a girl by the name of Nancy Hanks who lived at the home of Abraham Enloe on Puzzle Creek, in Rutherford County.

She made the statement many times that she had seen Nancy and her child at the old Enloe home-place; and that it was the belief of all the old people that the child was born there and later was taken to some place in Kentucky.

My great-grandmother said that Enloe hired Tom Lincoln to marry this girl, and was to give him "fifty dollars and a team."

At the conclusion of Rev. Smart's story, he gave as his reason for so definitely remembering what his great-grandmother had said, that about two years before she died a Methodist minister by the name of C.R. Lee, of Cliffside, N.C. came to see this old lady to secure information about Lincoln's origin, which he was writing up for some paper. This preacher stayed in the community two or three weeks, getting this information, and Mr. Smart was then about fifteen years old and heard this old lady make these statements a number of times to Rev. Lee.

State of North Carolina
County of Rutherford

Personally appeared before me this the 8th day of December, 1926, B.B. Smart, who being first duly sworn, deposes and says: That he is the author of the foregoing story, that he has read the foregoing story, and that the matters therein stated are true of his own knowledge, except as to those matters stated on information and belief, and as to those matters he believes it to be true.

Sworn to and subscribed before me this the 8th day of December, 1926.

B.B. Smart
E.E. Harrill, Notary Public
My commission expires December 22, 1926

Story By George DePriest

Mr. George DePriest, of Shelby, N.C., an old gentleman seventy-two years old, gave the following story:

He said, that when he was living in the community of Duncan's Creek, Rutherford County, he was well acquainted with an old lady by the name of Polly Price, popularly called "Aunt Polly," who lived to be a hundred years old. He says he often saw "Aunt Polly" and talked to her, and she told Mr. DePriest about her association in her girlhood with a girl by the name of "Nancy Hanks" who came to see her and danced at her home at quiltings, and she went to the home of Nancy Hanks, where she lived at Abraham Enloe's on Puzzle Creek, and danced there. She said she lived about ten miles from Enloe's, and often visited Nancy there.

"Aunt Polly" said she saw Nancy Hanks after her child was born at the old Enloe home, from which the Enloe family had moved a short while before to the mountains. And she also saw her at the old "Concord Baptist Church," where she took the baby from Nancy and held him in her arms. "And when Nancy got ready to leave for Kentucky," Aunt Polly said, "she was at the old Enloe place, and I saw her get on a horse behind a man who was a 'horse trader' and ride away, the man taking the baby in his arms."

Mr. DePriest says he was reared in that same neighborhood, and that "beyond the shadow of a doubt Abraham Enloe was the father of Abraham Lincoln."

State of North Carolina
County of Cleveland

Personally appeared before me this 8th day of December, 1926, G.W. DePriest, who being duly sworn, deposes and says: That he is the author of the foregoing story, that he has read the foregoing story and that the matters therein stated are true of his own knowledge, except as to those matters stated on information and belief and as to those matters he believes it to be true.

G.W. DePriest

Sworn to and subscribed before me, this the 8th day of December, 1926.

A.M. Hamrick
Clerk Superior Court

Story By Attorney C.O. Ridings

Mr. C.O. Ridings of Forest City, a leading lawyer of that place, furnished the following interesting story:

He says that he is the grandson of the late Hon. Columbus Tanner of this Rutherford County, North Carolina, and who for more than eighteen years was Clerk of the Superior Court of Rutherford County. He says his grandfather was born in the year 1839, and died in 1923, and knew all of the old people well who were conversant with the facts in this case about Nancy Hanks.

Mr. Columbus Tanner spent considerable time in getting up all the facts, says Mr. Ridings, and writing a brief history of the matter, in which he hung Nancy Hanks on the Tanner family tree, claiming that Michael Tanner (Columbus Tanner's uncle) was the father of Nancy by Lucy Hanks.

In his grandfather's write-up, says Mr. Ridings, it was stated that the girl, Nancy Hanks, stayed at Abraham Enloe's, on Puzzle Creek; and that the child later known as Abraham Lincoln was born there.

"That a horse-trader by the name of Michael Tanner took Nancy on his horse behind him and carried her away with the baby in his arms. Abraham Enloe was believed to be the father of the child," said Mr. Tanner in this manuscript written about sixty years ago (now 1935).

Mr. Tanner's manuscript has been lost or misplaced, but the attorney, Mr. Ridings, says he read this old manuscript as many as three times and knows its contents, and besides this he says he heard his grandfather relate the same many times.

Mr. Ridings' mother, daughter of Columbus Tanner, said to this writer that she well remembered passing along the road between where Bostic and Forest City are located, when she was a little girl, in company with her grandfather, and at some point near where Bostic is located her grandfather pointed North and said, "Right out there about a mile and a half is where Abraham Lincoln was born"!

State of North Carolina
County of Rutherford

Personally appeared before me this the 3rd day of December, C.O. Ridings, who being duly sworn deposes and says: That he is the author of the foregoing story; that he has read the foregoing story and that the matters therein stated are true of his own knowledge, except as to those matters stated on information and belief, and as to those matters he believes it to be true.

C.O. Ridings

Sworn to and subscribed before me this the 3rd day of December, 1926.

> D. L. Brown, Notary Public
> My commission expires March 22, 1927

Story by J. N. Jones

Mr. Jones is a leading merchant of Forest City. He said he was 62 years old and was reared in Rutherford County, and was familiar with the story of Nancy Hanks and her child, as told by the old people who knew the facts.

He says he lived near the old lady called "Grannie" Hollifield, and talked with her frequently. He says she lived to be over a hundred years old, and he often heard her say that she had held Abraham Lincoln in her arms when he was a babe; that he was born at the old Abraham Enloe place on Puzzle Creek, in Rutherford County, N.C.

State of North Carolina
County of Rutherford

Personally appeared before me this the 4th day of December, 1926, J. N. Jones, who being first duly sworn deposes and says: that he is the author of the foregoing story; that he has read the foregoing story, and that the matters therein stated are true of his own knowledge, except as to the matters stated on information and belief and as to those matters he believes it to be true.

> J. N. Jones

Sworn to and subscribed before me this the 4th day of December, 1926.

> W. L. Brown, Notary Public
> My commission expires March 22, 1927

Story by A. DeK. Wallace

Mr. Wallace is seventy-eight years old. He is called the best historian in Rutherford County. He is a well educated man and has been very prominent in the life and development of the county. This old man knew personally the old people who saw the girl, Nancy Hanks, before and after her child was born.

He says Michael Tanner was the father of Nancy Hanks, and that Daniel Tanner was her half-brother. And he says he received this information from William A. Tanner, one of Rutherford County's most prominent men.

Nancy was placed in the home of Abraham Enloe, on Puzzle Creek, he says, when she was a small girl and grew to womanhood in this Enloe family. When she was about grown she became the mother of a child and Abraham Enloe was considered its father, and the child was called "Abe" for him.

After this, the girl and child were both sent to Kentucky, and later the girl married a man there by the name of Tom Lincoln.

"When I was a small boy," says Mr. Wallace, "I heard some of the old people talking something about 'lynching' Abraham Enloe, though I never understood why they talked about lynching him."

State of North Carolina
County of Rutherford

Personally appeared before me this the 4th day of December, 1926, A. DeK. Wallace, who being first duly sworn deposes and says: That he is the author of the foregoing story; that he has read the foregoing story and the matters therein stat- ed are true of his own knowledge, except as to those matters stated on information and belief and as to those matters he believes it to be true.

A. DeK. Wallace

Sworn to and subscribed before me this the 4th day of

December, 1926.

Alice Greer, Notary Public
My commission expires April 20, 1926

Story by Edmond Dills

Mr. Dills is 78 years old; he is from Jackson County, near where Abraham Enloe settled. He says:

When Nancy Hanks was missed from the home of Abraham Enloe by the neighbors, the citizens thought that Enloe had taken this girl off and killed her. They said he was gone about six weeks from his home, and finally he returned without her. Nobody knew where he had been all this time. The feeling grew among the people and they began to talk about visiting upon him severe punishment. But just about the time that had been set for a reckoning with him, the report came that Nancy was alive and was the mother of a child. The old people all said its name ought to have been Enloe, for it was the general understanding that Abraham Enloe was its father.

State of North Carolina
County of Rutherford

Personally appeared before me this the 10th day of December, 1926, Davis Edmond Dill, who being first duly sworn deposes and says: That he is the author of the foregoing story; that he has read the foregoing story and that the matters therein stated are true of his own knowledge, except as to those matters stated on information and belief and as to those matters he believes it to be true.

Clifford C. Crow, J.P.

Sworn to and subscribed before me this the 10th day of December, 1926.

Story of Mrs. Martha Keeter

Mrs. Martha Keeter is 78 years old, and was born and reared in Rutherford County, North Carolina. She was a Bradley, daughter of the late Willis Bradley. She says she often heard her father speak of Nancy Hanks and Abraham Lincoln.

She always heard, she says, that Lincoln was born in Rutherford County, and knew nothing to the contrary until she was a grown woman. Her father knew all of the old associates of Nancy Hanks. He said Nancy was raised in the family of Abraham Enloe, and that Abraham Lincoln was born in Rutherford County, and he and his mother were carried to Kentucky by a "horse-trader."

She said Willis Bradley was a well-to-do man and owned a goodly number of slaves. But he was a great friend of President Lincoln, and believed in the policies of Lincoln who was then a "Whig."

Mr. Bradley was frequently taunted by members of the opposite party, who said, "Lincoln was an illegitimate"; and there was no way of answering this charge, for the old people all knew this to be a fact, said Mrs. Keeter. "But Lincoln was not personally responsible for what his parents or somebody else did before he was born," her father often said.

Willis Bradley was born in 1805, and died in 1904. (This story calls to mind the fact that Mr. Lincoln got only three votes in his home county in Kentucky, and the reason assigned was that the people said at the election that he was a "bastard." They made the same charge at the polls in North Carolina that they did in Kentucky.)

State of North Carolina
County of Rutherford

    Personally appeared before me this the 3rd day of December, 1926, Mrs. Martha Keeter, who first being duly sworn deposes and says: That she is the author of the foregoing story; that she has read the foregoing story and that the matters stated therein are true of her own knowledge, except as to those matters stated on information and belief and as to those matters she believes it to be true.

Mrs. Martha Keeter

Sworn to and subscribed before me this the 3rd day of December, 1926.

Alice Greer, Notary Public
My commission expires April 20, 1928

Story by General Theodore Davidson

General Davidson is a member of the oldest law firm in the City of Asheville, North Carolina; one of the leading and most highly esteemed citizens of the State, for eight years Attorney General of North Carolina and for a number of years a member of the General Assembly of the State. No man stands higher. He said (in 1928):

Some fifteen or twenty years ago a lady from Illinois was traveling through our mountain country and decided to spend the summer here. She went to Bryson City to stop at the hotel and found the hotel crowded. Upon the suggestion of the proprietor of the hotel she applied at a nearby cottage, where she was very cordially received and was given a comfortable room.

Being shown into the sitting room, she amused herself by examining the pictures and various decorations on the wall of the room. Among others was a large size photograph of a strong and unusually striking appearance. When the hostess returned to the room her new guest said, "Aren't you a Southerner?" "Yes." "And I presume are Democrats?" asked the lady. "Yes, of the strongest sect," was the immediate reply. "Then," said the traveling lady, "What do you mean?" Whereupon the lady pointed to the large photograph, saying, "I have seen Mr. Lincoln, and am familiar with his features and appearance, and that is as good a picture of him as I ever saw."

"Why," said the hostess, "that is not a picture of Abe Lincoln; that is a picture of my grandfather, Wesley Enloe, who was born, lived and died on the old Abraham Enloe place on Ocona Lufta, in this, Swain, County, North Carolina."

In connection with the above statement the old General said: "I was born in the vicinity of this Enloe tradition, as was my father before me. My father and I settled the Enloe estate."

"Mr. Coggins, the story IS true! it is TRUE!" the old General said, very emphatically. Following up the above story, General Davidson said that a New York paper sent a reporter down to interview the Enloe family in regard to the tradition, and the members of the family decided that before anything was reported they had better get together and talk this matter over just among themselves.

They had a meeting and talked it over and the decision was that there was nothing that they could say, pro or con, and their refusal to be interviewed was understood to be a silent acknowledgment of the truthfulness of the story.

Story by Preston Bostic

Preston Bostic says he is 52 years old. His father, McBryer Bostic, bought the old Enloe farm on Puzzle Creek when he was a young man. Mr. Bostic says, when he was a very small boy, he and his father stopped on a trip to South Carolina and stayed over night with an old man at Clifton, in South Carolina, who had been raised on Puzzle Creek, near the old Enloe farm.

This man was a Mr. Wilkie, a very old gentleman who said he had worked for Mr. Enloe when he was a boy on a Puzzle Creek farm, and personally knew the Enloe family and the girl, Nancy Hanks, who stayed with the Enloes. They stayed up until midnight, said Bostic, talking about the Enloes, Nancy Hanks and her child.

The old man related an incident which happened in the Enloe family, corroborating our Rutherford County story, in some very interesting points.

He told about the runaway marriage of a daughter of Abraham Enloe. He said that there were two Enloe girls about grown, and Nancy Hanks was just about grown at that time.

Mr. Enloe had gone off on a trip and was away from home, and one of his girls ran off and got married. The couple went up Puzzle Creek about two miles to where a preacher lived by the name of Swable, who performed the ceremony for them. Then the couple left for the "West," and their first stop was at Joe Green's, the man who kept the post office on the road or trail toward Chimney Rock.

Nancy Hanks went to Rev. Swable's with the runaway couple, and when she came back and told Mrs. Enloe they were married, Mrs. Enloe was greatly worried over it and took on terribly.

She sent for this Mr. Wilkie who lived near, and had him go in search of Abraham Enloe. After some time Wilkie found him at what was then called "The Red Tavern," on the road between where Spindale and Forest City are now located.

Enloe was on a spree, and was telling jokes, and when he was told that his daughter had run off and got married, he didn't seem to care very much. But he was soon ready to go home. On the way back, when they came to Second Broad River, they encountered great difficulty in crossing the river as the bridge was gone and the log also on which Wilkie had "cooned it" on his way to the tavern. They had no light, it was dark and raining, and they had to feel their way along the river bank trying to find a place to cross.

After failing to find any way to cross the river, which was now rising on account of recent rains, Abraham Enloe, a very large, tall and sinewy man weighing between two and three hundred pounds, turned to Wilkie and said, "I am going across!" And he told Wilkie to get on his back and he would carry him across the river. The plan worked admirably, for Enloe being very tall and with Wilkie to weigh him down to keep him from washing down the stream, they were able to keep their heads above the water until they had reached the other side.

When they reached home they found Mrs. Enloe down stairs, crying, and Nancy Hanks with her, and the other girl, Enloe's other daughter, was up stairs singing and dancing.

After warming by a good fire, Wilkie told Mr. Enloe that they were out of bread at his house and Enloe went to the grainery and got a bushel of wheat and Wilkie took it to Baxter's mill that night and had it ground.

The next morning there was a big snow on the ground. Wilkie went up to Enloe's, and Enloe asked him to go with him hunting. They started out walking, the snow being about half-leg deep, and they had gone just a little way when they ran across deer tracks. They followed this trail a short distance to a small strip of woods between two branches. Here two deer jumped up and stood side-by-side looking at them. Enloe said, "Let's shoot," and at the crack of the guns one deer fell and the other leaped off, leaving blood on the snow. They shouldered the deer that was killed and took it to the house and dressed it.

Enloe insisted that they had killed both deer. So they soon started in pursuit of the other. They saw by the constant flow of blood on the snow that it was badly wounded, and after they had followed it about a half mile they came to a neighbor's house and found where the deer had been skinned. They said they thought they smelled some of it cooking, and called and sure enough they had some of it in the pot boiling.

These folks said the deer came to their house and fell dead in the yard, and they offered to let Enloe and Wilkie have it, but they took one hind quarter and the hide, leaving the rest for the neighbor where the deer died.

Days passed and nothing was heard from the "runaway couple." Nancy Hanks would go to the post office on horse-back and ask for mail, but no word was received, and the Enloes were getting very much worried about their missing daughter. About the twelfth day Nancy Hanks got on a horse and went after the mail again. She was not gone so long this time. They heard her coming, singing (she was a good singer), and as she came up to the house she was patting the horse on the neck and held up a letter from the runaways. They had gone to Tennessee or Kentucky, and were settled in a home of their own.

State of North Carolina
County of Rutherford

Personally appeared before me this the 3rd day of December, 1926, L. V. Bostic, who being first duly sworn deposes and says: That he is the author of the foregoing story; that he has read the foregoing story and that the matters therein stated are true of his own knowledge, except as to those matters stated upon information and belief and as to those matters he believes it to be true.

L. V. Bostic

Sworn to and subscribed before me this the 3rd day of December, 1926.

S. C. Gettys, Notary Public
My commission expires August 27, 1928

Most of these foregoing stories were secured by me for my second edition of the book, *Abraham Lincoln, a North Carolinian*. And it will be noted that the actual birthplace of Lincoln is definitely located by these affidavits. And while it has been said by the historians, that "one affidavit is just as good as another," yet the serious reader will note this difference:

That these affidavits do not disagree among themselves, as do the affidavits secured by the various apologists. Here is harmony and correlation, and on the other hand there is confusion! Here is but one birth-place; in Kentucky there are eleven! With four log cabins! And twenty "Nancy Hankses, with the wrong fathers and mothers!" Verily, "the legs of the lame are not equal!"

Story by David Hyde of Stecoah, Graham County, N. C.

David Hyde of Graham County, died February 4th, 1930,

being 95 years and eight months old, this writer conducting the funeral at a nearby country cemetery. This old gentleman was a prominent pioneer citizen of this county, having served the county as Sheriff, Magistrate and school teacher. He was in full possession of his mental powers until the day of his death.

Mr. Hyde said:

> My father, John Hyde, Bob Collins and John Plott hunted deer, bear and panthers together in the Smokey Mountains with large dogs called "Plott dogs." Abraham Enloe had the same kind of dogs, sometimes called "Mastiffs." These fine dogs would catch anything; and they were trained to run bear and other big game. A panther killed a child upon Lufty and carried it off and ate it, and the neighbors sent for the Plott dogs at once. And the dogs immediately took the trail of the Panther and followed in hot pursuit, every dog running at full speed and yelping at each jump – it was a great race! The panther was making for its den in the Cataloochie Mountains, but the Plott dogs were too fast for the beast, though he was a fast running animal, and overtook him before he reached his den and forced him to go utj a tree. Here the dogs jumped up barking, growling and gnawing the bark on the big tree until the men came on with their guns and shot the vicious murderer of the child.

Then, after his interesting panther story, he said:

> My father worked for Abraham Enloe, on Ocona Lufta River, when he was a boy; he knew the girl Nancy Hanks, the mother of Abraham Lincoln, before she was sent off from the Enloe home. He knew the circumstances that led to the unpleasant gossip and family trouble in Enloe's home, and he related these things to me.
>
> Nancy was sent away somewhere in the care of a man by the name of Felix Walker, and it was not long until news came that Nancy was the mother of a child, and it was generally understood that Enloe was his father. Nobody in the community knew where the girl went, or where the baby was born. Enloe had some folks living in Kentucky who came in on a visit and they took Nancy and the child back with them, where she married a man by

name of Thomas Lincoln who was a distiller, and the child took his name.

Mr. Enloe was a good man, a man looked up to as a leader in his community. He was good to the poor. No man ever came to him for help and was turned away; he did a great deal of reading for the community. Many people were not able to read, and Enloe was a well educated man for his day. He was a Magistrate and tried all the cases in that part of the country. In all these cases, he tried to settle the troubles without a trial if it was possible, but if this was impossible he was firm and immovable for what he thought was right. When this trouble came up, it was said that he refused to read or to try any more cases.

CHAPTER FOUR

Magazine and Newspaper Endorsement

It has been claimed by at least one member of the "Historical School" that "no article appeared earlier than 1872 which threw any doubt upon the legitimacy of Abraham Lincoln" (Barton). But the same author had in his possession then, and quoted the history of the late James Cathey, a Lincoln Historian, whose book contains a reference to a newspaper article that was published in Tennessee, in 1861; and while we have no date of the publication of the newspaper at Mount Sterling, Kentucky, by the noted Judge Peters, we have reason to believe that his paper was published much earlier than "1872."

This distinguished Kentuckian, Judge Peters, began his law practice in 1827, and he made affidavit to the fact that "from the beginning of his legal practice to its close, covering a period of 60 years, he never came in contact with a Kentucky lawyer who doubted the illegitimacy of Abraham Lincoln"! They all disbelieved he was Tom Lincoln's son, and it was the general understanding that he was the son of Abraham Enloe.

Moreover, it came out in the newspapers during the famous Lincoln-Douglas campaign, that this tall sky-scraper who was snowing Judge Douglas under with his masterful logic, was not a Lincoln; but was known as "the son of Nancy Hanks." This appeared in the campaign papers, as will be noted in the story in this book by Mr. Crawford.

Article from *The Vindicator*

May 18, 1889, Rutherfordton, N.C.

Years ago, Col. G. Logan, now deceased, told the Editor of *The Vindicator*, that the first likeness he ever saw of Abraham Lincoln forcibly reminded him of Abraham Enloe, a citizen and Surveyor of Rutherford County; and that was before he ever heard of Lincoln's birth. When he heard the story, he was then confirmed in his belief that Abraham and Nancy were responsible for acts which led to the credit of Abe Lincoln's paternity.

And, while I am not free to make known the name of the prominent old gentleman whose confidential talk in a bank so strongly corroborated the above newspaper article, this Banker stated to me very emphatically that the above-named "Col. Albert Logan" told him that Abraham Lincoln and Abraham Enloe, formerly from Rutherford County, "were as much alike as two black-eyed peas"; that "the picture of one would easily pass for the picture of the other."

Lincoln's picture was in the papers during and after the famous "Lincoln-Douglas Campaign" in Illinois, and the people of Rutherford County had their attention called, frequently, to the very striking resemblance of this "candidate" to their friend and prominent citizen, Abraham Enloe, and reputed father of Lincoln. Of course this revived the old story about Mrs. Enloe's charges, and driving "Nancy Hanks" away from the Enloe home.

Dr. Chappel, Editor of *The National Magazine*, Boston, Gives Strong Editorial Endorsement to N.C. Tradition

Anything and everything that pertains to Abraham Lincoln is of world-wide interest. The very mention of the name "Lincoln" is becoming more and more magical in awakening the imagination as to the life of the man whose greatness, goodness and humanity will serve as a model for mankind for all time to come, for Lincoln truly belongs to the ages. Small wonder, then, at the keen interest manifested in Nancy Hanks, the mother of Lincoln, for did he not stand at her grave in manhood's estate and declare, "All that I am or may ever hope to be I owe to my mother"?

While visiting my friend, James W. Atkins, editor of the Gastonia, North Carolina *Gazette*, and speaking in those parts, he told me that Nancy Hanks once lived near Gastonia. This was enough. A pilgrimage was planned to visit the scenes and site of the cabin where Nancy Hanks spent her formative girlhood days and dreamed dreams – perhaps little dreaming that as she carried water from the spring to the log cabin home of her uncle, Dicky Hanks, that she was to become the mother of one of the greatest men who ever walked the earth.

On the banks of the Catawba River, in what is now known as Gaston County, lived an orphan girl who had come there from Amelia County, Virginia to live with an uncle who had pioneered with a brother and sister, establishing a home among the pines near a spring on the Catawba River. Many of his descendants still live in this locality, and from father and mother to children has come the story, in various versions, concerning Nancy Hanks.

The first of the family known in America was Benjamin Hanks, who landed in Massachusetts in 1669. One of the sons moved to Virginia. From the old town of Belmont we drove along the state road for some miles, and then turned abruptly to the left, on an old partially-abandoned, red-clay road leading on to an area of old fields among the second-growth pines. Leaving this road for another almost obliterated by vegetation, we came to a clump of pines not far from the river, and walked for some distance until we came to a lonely deserted area on the crest of a hill just above a spring that was still bubbling forth the waters that Nancy Hanks carried in pails to the cabin.

Mrs. Pruet of Belmont, a daughter of Mr. Stowe who owned the farm, born in this locality, said that her father erected the monument to mark the spot so closely associated with the life of the mother of Lincoln. He had heard the story and neighborhood gossip since boyhood, verified by living witnesses, and felt

Nancy's Log-Cabin Home in North Carolina

Down near the banks of the Catawba River, near Belmont, N. C., stands yet the little old log cabin in which Lincoln's mother lived with her uncle "Dick" (Richard), for some years after being brought as an "orphan" from Virginia. She was a child of mystery. And the descendants of the Tanner family which came from Germany in 1750 held the secret of Nancy's ancestry.

that he should place a marker upon the cabin which sheltered Nancy Hanks, as second in importance to that cabin which sheltered her babe, Abraham Lincoln, in old Hardin County, Kentucky.

Nancy Hanks left her uncle's home here while he still resided on the Catawba, and went to live in the western part of what was then Lincoln County, now Rutherford County, near where the town of Rutherfordton is today. Here she lived in the home of Abraham Enloe, going there for the purpose of assisting Mrs. Enloe with her household duties. She later went with this family to what is now Swain County, North Carolina.

That Nancy Hanks lived here and that part of her subsequent life was spent in North Carolina, were well known and undisputed in this community.

On the face of this monument, which is of massive granite, is a bronze tablet bearing a replica of a log cabin and the following inscription: "This stone marks the site of the log cabin of Dicky Hanks, an uncle of Nancy Hanks, mother of Abraham Lincoln. Nancy spent much of her childhood here with her uncle."

The foundation stones on which the boulder was placed were once part of the chimney of the original cabin. The logs of this cabin, rough-hewn from virgin timber, have endured to this day, according to family tradition.

At the foot of the hill on which was set the simple home in the primeval forest, is a bubbling spring. A lone beech tree stands guard over it.

Historians' accounts as to the paternity of Nancy Hanks differ greatly. Ida M. Tarbell, in her *Life of Lincoln*, skips over the life of this woman with only a few words. Along with the other writers who have treated the early life of Abraham Lincoln's ancestors, she tells of Nancy Hanks' relation to Joseph Hanks, of Virginia and Kentucky. Joseph Hanks left a will in which disposition is made of his property to his living relatives. No mention, however, is made of the name of Dicky Hanks in this will, a facsimile of which is shown in Miss Tarbell's work.

William H. Herndon, a native of Springfield, Illinois, who

was intimately connected with Lincoln in long years of political life, produced a work that does go back into some of the traditions surrounding the life of Nancy Hanks.

He tells of riding with Lincoln through Illinois, in a buggy. He asked his companion something of his parentage. Contrary to his usual custom, Lincoln spoke freely of a subject that he preferred not to discuss. He said, with a degree of sadness, that his mother was the illegitimate daughter of Lucy Hanks, and he ascribed his traits of character and mental characteristics, totally unlike those possessed by the other Lincolns and Hankses, to that of his unknown grandfather whom he supposed to be a Virginia planter.

President Ganes Bears Testimony

This evidence is taken from this author's second edition on *Abraham Lincoln, a North Carolinian.*

About the year 1880, this North Carolina tradition was critically investigated by Dr. Tilman R. Ganes, a Baptist minister and writer of note. Dr. Ganes founded a college at Shelby, North Carolina, and became its first president. Because of his "broad culture and profound intellect," he made an indelible impression upon the Shelby people. Being in the immediate vicinity of the "Nancy Hanks" tradition, President Ganes decided to go into this matter for his own personal satisfaction, and he found so much startling material that he published a lengthy series of articles in the Shelby *Aurora*.

Mr. J.R. Quinn, for many years Postmaster at Shelby, gave us this information. Mr. Quinn says he well remembers Dr. Ganes, who preached for the Baptist church in Shelby and was the president of the college. He stated that Rev. Ganes was endowed with the most wonderful intellect of any man he had ever seen, and his newspaper articles were still remembered by him because they were so radically different from anything he had ever seen.

But Prof. Ganes ran across the trail of the Nancy Hanks tradition and went into it with the persistence of a bloodhound.

He carefully investigated these stories, following them to their various sources. To make sure that he was correct in his diagnosis, he went to Kentucky and made a careful survey of the most authentic sources of information to be found in that State. After sifting out the chaff from the wheat he found that North Carolina had a very much stronger claim to the birthplace of Abraham Lincoln than Kentucky. Mr. Ganes claimed that he had discovered evidence which proved beyond a reasonable doubt that "Honest Abe" was born in Rutherford County, North Carolina. He looked up the old people who were in position to guide him to the spot, and they took him to "Lincoln Hill" on Puzzle Creek. And they pointed to this old rock basement on the hill as the unmistakable site of Lincoln's birthplace. This was the position that he took in his newspaper articles, which are remembered yet by a goodly number of the people in this section of the country. I made a trip to Shelby to see if I could find a copy of the paper containing his article, but was informed that they had been destroyed by fire some years ago. However, I am yet hoping to find a copy that has been kept by someone who was taking this paper at that time.

This writer has talked to people who were members of the party that guided Dr. Ganes to the Lincoln birthplace.

Editorial Endorsements

Jas. P. Cook

Mr. James P. Cook, Editor of *The Uplift*, says in the issue of November 20, 1926, "There is scarcely any doubt of the accuracy of the contention of the minister of Rutherford County, who is quoted by Editor R. E. Price of the Rutherford County *News*."

This is by no means a late discovery. Several years prior to the death of the late General Julian S. Carr, it was the privilege of *The Uplift* to carry a story of "Lincoln and His Mother," which was compiled from a book in the General's library.

That story is in harmony with Editor Price's. Mr. Price, however, fails to tell of the visits of Nancy Hanks she was accustomed to make to her friends in Gaston County.

The above editorial endorsement came from Mr. Cook in answer to Mr. Price's article which recently appeared in the daily newspapers announcing that "Abraham Lincoln was born in Rutherford County, North Carolina," in which Editor Price gave a lengthy report of our meeting out at "Lincoln Hill."

"Nancy Hanks, Her Home In North Carolina"

We are here quoting an article which was furnished to the papers in 1910 by Mrs. Minnie Stowe Puett and Mrs. Adelaide Smith Beard. This is consistent with other stories which are found in Rutherford County. The apparent discrepancy is that Nancy was an orphan when she was brought from Virginia. But many a child has been called an "orphan" under similar circumstances. Mr. Warren digs up a Kentucky Court record showing that Nancy was not an orphan in 1789. And her mother was married to Henry Sparrow in Kentucky in 1791. So, according to documentary testimony, Nancy occupies the status which the North Carolina tradition claims she held at that time.

He is truly great who rises to greatness from profound obscurity.

There is no more wonderful truth in history than this statement, as the lives of many of the world's greatest men have borne witness. As Romulus and Remus came from the lair of the wolf to become the founders of immortal Rome; as the great Napoleon arose from his humble Corsican cottage to be the ruler of Europe; so Abraham Lincoln lifted himself from a pioneer cabin to a place of supreme greatness that is magnified as the years roll by.

His origin and rise to immortality embodies in itself as has the life of no other person, the true spirit of American democracy. This principle has been ignored by the majority of historians, who have seemingly deemed it necessary to manufacture from their own imaginations an origin worthy of his greatness. This fallacy is all too unnecessary, for the position that Lincoln now occupies in the hall of fame is secure beyond their ability to add to or to detract therefrom.

Little has ever been written concerning Nancy Hanks, Lincoln's mother; and the fact that she spent most of her early life in North Carolina has been unknown or ignored by his biographers. In an effort to "preserve this truth to history" there has recently been erected near the town of Belmont, Gaston County, North Carolina, a monument on the site where stood her cabin home, near the banks of the Catawba.

The silver current of this river wends its way slowly through the verdant hills. From its mountain sources of ice-cold springs, winning tribute from a thousand rills, it reigns a queenly river, matchless in its beauty and wonderful in its power. Along its flower-enameled borders the dark brown Indians roamed in the years gone by. Sapona, the great chief of the Catawbas, lighted his council fires on its banks. The Indians have gone forever, but their fame is kept immortal by the river which bears their name.

The beauty and fertility of the Catawba valley attracted many of the early settlers to this region, and their primitive homes were built on the hills overlooking the stream. In one of these little cabins lived a maiden whose name and life were destined to become of vital importance and enduring fame throughout the nation. She is described as having dark hair, sallow complexion, and gray eyes, and of sad and thoughtful countenance. Little else is known of her personality, but all the world knows her as Nancy Hanks, the mother of Abraham Lincoln.

According to local tradition (Gaston County) Nancy Hanks was an orphan and came to North Carolina with her uncle, Dicky Hanks, when he moved here from Virginia. The first member of the Hanks family about whom anything is known was Benjamin Hanks, who came to Massachusetts from England in 1699. One of his sons, William Hanks, moved to Virginia. He had a family of twelve children, his descendants forming a large settlement in Amelia County, some of his family migrated to Kentucky, while others came to North Carolina.

Three members of the Hanks family, two uncles and an aunt of Nancy Hanks, settled in Lincoln, now Gaston County, North Carolina, near the beginning of the nineteenth century. They were accompanied from Virginia by the "orphan," Nancy, who spent most of her girlhood here with one of these uncles,

"Dicky" Hanks. He was the ancestor of many of the present residents of Gaston and Lincoln Counties. He moved away from his home on the Catawba and lived in another part of the county where he was afterwards burned to death. Much stress is laid by some historians on the will of one, Joseph Hanks, of Virginia and Kentucky, claiming that the Lucy Hanks named in his will, was the mother of Nancy Hanks Lincoln. This could not have been true, since it is positively known that Dicky Hanks was Nancy's uncle and there is no Dicky or Richard Hanks mentioned in Joseph's will.

Nancy left her uncle's home while he still resided on the Catawba, and went to live in the western part of what was then Lincoln, now Rutherford County, North Carolina, near where the town of Rutherfordton stands today. Here she lived in the home of Abraham Enloe, going there for the purpose of assisting Mrs. Enloe with her household duties. She, later went with this family to what is now Swain County, North Carolina.

Abraham Enloe is described as being of a fine physique, tall, angular, with dark skin and coarse black hair. He was a leader in his community, being a man of naturally keen intellect and having an education much superior to his associates. His father was a school teacher and came to this country from Scotland and personally educated his son. While Nancy was an inmate of the Enloe home, circumstances arose which caused Mrs. Enloe to insist that she be sent away; she was taken to Kentucky by a relative of the family, whose home was in that State. These facts have been always known in the communities where she lived, in Gaston, Rutherford and Swain counties, and many of the present members of the Enloe family acknowledge their truth.

The boulder pictured in this article was recently erected by the descendants of a former owner of the land on which it stands. He personally remembered the cabin and often pointed out this site as the home of Nancy and Dickey Hanks. That Nancy lived here and her subsequent life in North Carolina were both well known and undisputed in this community. On the face of this boulder, which is of massive granite, is a bronze tablet bearing a replica of a frontier cabin and the following inscription: "This stone marks the site of the log cabin home of Dicky Hanks, uncle of Nancy Hanks, mother of Abraham Lincoln. Nancy spent much of her girlhood here with her uncle." The foundation stones on which the boulder was placed were once part of the chimney of the original cabin. The logs of this cabin, rough hewn from virgin timber, have endured until today, and according to family tradition then were rebuilt into another cabin still in use on this plantation.

At the foot of the hill on which was set this simple home, in the primeval forest, is a bubbling spring. A lone beech tree today stands guard over it. Can we not imagine the young Nancy wending her way down the hill to this quiet spot, where she quenched her thirst with the sparkling waters and searched its hidden depths for her mirrored reflection?

On viewing the magnificent monument which the nation recently erected on the Potomac at Washington, to suitably commemorate the great Lincoln, let one thought be given the woman who shaped his young life, to Nancy Hanks, his mother.

These witnesses and writers are people of very superior and "brilliant intellect" who had no sinister motives to be indulged, no axe to grind; but who only desired the unvarnished truth in this case.

CHAPTER FIVE

A Recent Discovery

We are now entering upon our task with a profound consciousness that we are offering a surprise to every reader of this book who will follow us with an open mind, as free from bias as the juryman who has taken his oath to listen to the testimony and at the conclusion render his verdict according to the evidence in the case.

And every one who values the truth owes this to himself. I say this because of the known fact that we have taken up the unpopular side of this unsettled question; the side so unpopular that we have more than once been advised that we better not write this book, that it would hurt us if we should do this. But the first Lincoln historians encountered this same unpleasant difficulty.

The recent discovery of an old manuscript has brought to light a very profound family secret in regard to the birth and ancestry of Nancy Hanks, the mother of President Lincoln. This secret was faithfully kept for many years in a very prominent and wealthy family whose ancestors came to this country directly from Germany in the 18th century (1750), and settled in Virginia. It shows a close correspondence to Lincoln's statement to his law partner, Herndon, that his (Lincoln's) "mother was an illegitimate daughter of Lucy Hanks and a Virginian of very fine blood." And members of this high-class family "of good German blood" have laid claim to a close kinship to Lincoln, known only among themselves for over a hundred years, until recently discovered.

This secret was preserved for many years in manuscript form, having been written for the family only, and showing the family relationship to Abraham Lincoln through Nancy Hanks the daughter of Lucy Hanks and a member of this prominent German family.

I made this discovery while sitting in a lawyer's office at Forest City, North Carolina, getting the material for my second edition of the book, *Abraham Lincoln, a North Carolinian*. This lawyer was a grandson of the old Judge who had written the matter up for the family; and I not only secured this lawyer's affidavit that he had seen and read the secret manuscript, but also that he had heard his grandfather relate the same a number of times. All of which will appear in this book.

But, after the publication of that book, showing the relationship as revealed in the manuscript written many years ago by this prominent member of this German family, I was, in the same neighborhood, treated to another surprise fully equal to the first which took place in the office of the lawyer.

Two Old Manuscripts Show Lincoln's German Blood

A farmer who had married into this German family told me about an old manuscript his wife's grandmother had prepared in Texas many years ago, setting forth this same relationship. And I called upon the family and secured the old lady's manuscript for this book. But the larger manuscript written by the old Judge having been misplaced or secretly carried off by some member of the family, I was not able to get; all I could do was to get the affidavit in regard to the contents of the old "book manuscript" showing Lincoln's relationship to this family.

An important item disclosed in the "book manuscript" was that Nancy Hanks was born at "some place in Amelia County, Virginia," and while yet an infant was brought by her own father in company with a number of other pioneers to Rutherford County, North Carolina, where they established settlements or bought land and built homes.

Among those who came from Virginia at this time was an uncle of Nancy Hanks who was known as "Dick" or Richard, Hanks, and who built a small log cabin on the Catawba River near the present town of Belmont, North Carolina.

It was, for some unaccountable reason, not brought out in either manuscript, at her uncle Richard's little one-room cabin home, that little Nancy spent a few years of her childhood. And during this time she was often spoken of as an "orphan" by the people of the community.

The theory that this girl was an orphan was based upon the information given out by the child's father, who had it put into the old record of the family, and which was held as a family secret. But I have a different theory. This child was not an "orphan," for her mother, Lucy Hanks, did not "die" when this child was born, as stated in the old manuscript; and it is stated that her father soon "married again."

Here is a strange discrepancy that might cause some to consider the whole story a fabrication; but under a critical analysis one will be able to detect the probable reason for this; it was a kind of ruse or stratagem, a deceptive trick, to cover up a scandal in the family "of good blood." It was an effort to cover up the "illegitimacy" of this child by members of this aristocratic family, formerly from Germany. They tried to keep this baby which was sired by the full German Michael Tanner. But this would not work in this country. And in a short time this "orphan" girl and its own mother, Lucy Hanks, not "Mrs. Tanner," are staying at the home of Richard Hanks down on the Catawba River, in North Carolina. There is abundant evidence to establish this fact, which will be offered later in this work.

The mother of this girl was a questionable character (Dr. Warren), and if she had been married in Virginia she remained with her husband there but a short while, and she failed to carry the name of her husband into North Carolina, where she resided for some time, after which she went to the State of Kentucky, where she married Henry Sparrow in 1790, but she was not called Tanner in Kentucky.

Nancy's uncle "Dick" (Richard) Hanks, with whom this little girl lived for a while, was a man of dissolute character, it is said by the old people. He would spend every dollar he could get for liquor and, stayed drunk nearly all the time. And he was put in jail at Rutherfordton and was compelled to work at his trade, making shoes, for the support of the family, after which he was accidentally burned to death (B.H. Melton).

Now there stands a lasting monument at the old "Dick" Hanks place, down on the Catawba River, erected to the memory of Lincoln's mother near the town of Belmont. And here stands yet the little old log cabin in which Lincoln's mother lived when she was a child in the home of her uncle. She was very probably a "nullia fullia," or an "illegitimate" child, as was related by her noble and distinguished son, Abraham Lincoln, to William Herndon in 1850. Of course Lincoln got this confidential information from his mother who had learned about her ancestry after she became old enough to understand such a delicate situation.

The following manuscript furnishes the very strongest kind of evidence of the truthfulness of our story:

Michael Tanner Came From Germany To Virginia in 1750

He had two sons, Daniel and Michael. Michael's wife died at the birth of her first infant, Nancy Hanks. Daniel Tanner took it to raise with his children on condition that it was never to know its parentage while any of the parties lived.

As near as I can learn, Daniel Tanner and Michael left Virginia and came to Rutherford County, North Carolina, in the latter part of the 18th century. On the way over here Daniel Tanner's wife died, and he married again soon after arriving here. As he was a peculiar man, he kept no records.

Nancy Hanks was born in Virginia and came to North Carolina with Daniel Tanner, whom she thought to be her father.

She had a misfortune and was driven from home, and went back to Virginia (Kentucky), where she married Lincoln and was soon lost sight of.

Daniel Tanner was to tell the secret to his oldest son, William A. Tanner; and this he did, but it was war times and he did not want to know of it, as Lincoln, Nancy Hanks' son, was then the President.

After learning that Columbus Tanner kept the secret of Nancy Hanks' birth, I convinced him that I had as much right to know it as any one. Then he told me all I know.

My mother and Nancy Hanks were first cousins, and were reared in the same house. I suppose "Nancy Hanks" was her given name, as I can not learn of her having any other.

In after years her father, Michael Tanner, married a Miss Panter and I have lost sight of him.

I will now tell who I am. My mother was Martha Tanner, Daniel Tanner's daughter. I married William Wood, who died November, 1848. I am the youngest of eleven children, age 75.

I married John Rutherford Walker.

My mother's sister married Bob Nix, and died in 1852. On her death bed she expressed her regrets that she had anything to do with driving Nancy Hanks, her sister (cousin), from home.

It was always known in my father's family that we were akin. But I never knew whether she was my mother's sister or cousin until I learned who kept the secret.

Columbus Tanner was free to tell me after learning my father's age, born in 1791, who was old enough to know.

Corroboration appears in both manuscripts, and the reason is they were from the same source, the Hon. Columbus Tanner.

CHAPTER SIX

Abraham Lincoln's Ancestry Not "White Trash"

The contents of the above genealogical manuscript, representing the salient points in the old document written about seventy-five years ago, as a true narrative in which was given the "family secret," by the Hon. Columbus Tanner, is in itself a great discovery.

This throws light upon the following important matters:

(1) It settles the disputed question as to Lincoln's maternal ancestry; and without this material preserved by the Tanners the world never would have known anything about the "Virginia family of good blood," with which President Lincoln was related.

Eugenics absolutely demands a strong family on both sides, in order to be able to produce such a man as Abraham Lincoln. Such men cannot be reared like mushrooms. They must have an adequate mental foundation in their ancestry – a foundation which was not possible in any of the Hankses of this country. It took very rich, intellectual blood to provide in the offspring of Lucy Hanks just the necessary strength in the mental seed to be the mother of a man of Lincoln's type. The statement that "her mother died" when she (Nancy) was born was, probably, a camouflage to conceal her illegitimacy (Herndon). For her mother, Lucy Hanks, lived on and married Henry Sparrow in Kentucky.

And, while this child may have been kept in the home of Daniel Tanner for some time after arriving in North Carolina, she was soon taken, probably by her mother, Lucy Hanks, to the little log cabin home of "Dick" (Richard) Hanks, her mother's brother, on the bank of the Catawba River, where the granite monument now stands, in commemoration of Lincoln's mother.

Had she been a legitimate child of Michael Tanner, she would have worn that name and she would not have been sent off to live in the hovel of "Dick" Hanks, the drunkard. The Tanners wanted to keep this beautiful replica of German ancestry, but when Daniel arrived here "he soon married again," and probably his second wife objected to caring for an illegitimate in her home "with her own children," and that was the reason why she was sent away.

(2) This old manuscript settles the question as to where Lincoln's mother spent her girlhood days. Dr. Warren, a good historian, claims that the historians are unable to find Nancy in Kentucky. And this old writing clears up this question. This shows the reason why Nancy did not make her home in Kentucky with her own mother. This has been a great puzzle to all historians.

(3) It also clears up the question as to just which, of all the different "Nancy Hankses" recently discovered by the historians, was the actual mother of Abraham Lincoln. The last account we had, there were about twenty-five, all saying "Lo, here!" And four different log cabins where he was not born, in Kentucky.

(4) It also clarifies the atmosphere in regard to the unsettled question of Lincoln's "illegitimacy." The fact that "she had a misfortune and was driven from home" corroborates the strong stories from various sources which show that her son, who became the President, was born before she went to Kentucky, and long before she saw Tom Lincoln, the distiller. This verifies the statement often made, that "there was not a drop of Lincoln blood" in the President of this name. Eugenics show that he could not have been President if Tom Lincoln had been his father. He would have lacked the mental foundation.

The sire of Lincoln, like the sire of Nancy Hanks (Tanner),

must have been above the average in mentality. Mind does not come from clay. President Woodrow Wilson made an egregious and flagrant blunder, as expressed in his book *Division and Reunion* (page 216), when he stated that "Abraham Lincoln came from the poorest white trash of the South." This statement is untrue. Lincoln was not only the intellectual equal of Wilson, but his real ancestors would not have suffered if they had been stood up beside those of President Wilson or any other President. They, the records show, were the intellectual superiors of the people in the communities in which they lived, as will appear further on in this book. I have known some of the very finest diamonds to be taken out of trash piles, but just because the diamonds had a "bad environment" they were not "trash"! And if the diamonds had remained forever in the pile of no good "trash," they would have lost none of their quality. They could shine just as brightly in a big pile of trash as upon the sickly finger of a king. And so with Lincoln; he was nobody's "trash," and his intellect sparkled from the old mud-log fireplace where he learned to write on board shovels, on to the great battle of intellects when this tall sky scraper so completely snowed under with his masterful logic the proud Judge Douglas in their great political campaign.

Lincoln's Mother Was Not a Hanks

(5) The fifth and most pertinent point brought to light by this old writing is the fact that Lincoln's mother was not a "Hanks." It is a fact that the breeding will show for itself in people as it does in all animal life. And it is said by people who knew her that she was far above the ordinary. This higher grade of offspring resulted from amphimixis with a higher mental seed, that was contained in any ordinary people. The Tanner stock pulled up the Lucy Hanks stock to a much higher altitude and level than it had ever before attained.

This child, Nancy, feels differently, acts differently and doubtless entertains different hopes from those of her ordinary mother, Lucy Hanks.

Abraham Lincoln said of his mother, "She was highly intellectual by nature, had a strong memory, acute judgment, and was cool and heroic" (*Abraham Lincoln, a North Carolinian*, p. 89, by this author).

"Her understanding was considered something wonderful." John Hanks speaks reverently of her "high intellectual forehead, which he considered but the proper seat of faculties like hers. Compared with the mental poverty of her husband and relatives, her accomplishments were certainly very great" (Warren's quotation, id., p. 72).

This girl was a Tanner, and should have been called Nancy Tanner, instead of Nancy Hanks, since the lack of a brief ceremony could have no effect upon the nature or mentality inherited by the offspring. It was the Tanner in her personality that developed those peculiar marks of distinction mentioned by Lincoln and referred to by John Hanks and Herndon. There is no record of any other Hanks being "highly intellectual by nature," and whose understanding was "wonderful"; as "compared with the mental poverty of her husband and relatives." These are distinctive marks of her intellectual sire, the "Virginian of good blood," mentioned by Abraham Lincoln, her son.

Then, these old documents will forever settle the question of the ancestry of the girl who became the mother of Abraham Lincoln; her grandfather being Michael Tanner, Senior, and her father being Michael Junior. And the record was preserved for the family in writing; first by the Hon. Columbus Tanner, who for many years was Clerk or Judge of the Superior Court of Rutherford County, North Carolina. And it was his uncle Michael who was this girl's father. The second written document was by a daughter of Daniel Tanner, Michael's brother.

Moreover, the reader will also find, further on, the affidavit in support of these facts by Hon. C. O. Ridings, Attorney of Forest City, North Carolina, and grandson of Hon. Columbus Tanner. This is first-class historical matter that will stand the fire of all adverse criticism and will lay a permanent foundation for the intellectual ancestry of Lincoln's mother, furnishing her the mental ability to become the mother of a President of this great country.

Our position is made still more irrefutable from another old "record" used by the historian, Herndon, in defense of his position, that Nancy Hanks, the mother of Lincoln, was an illegitimate of very fine blood.

"A Remarkable Document"

Dr. William E. Barton, in his *Paternity* critique, insists that he did find a "remarkable document," which had been written by William Herndon "about the year 1866 to 1877." This work appears to be an answer or rebuttal to what Dennis Hanks had said as to the ancestry of "Nancy Hanks," the mother of Lincoln, says the historian. The writing shows that Dennis had been willing to side-step the truth, and Herndon, the historian, was drawing Dennis over the coals for misrepresenting the real truth, and which at that time was of "record" and in the possession of Herndon himself.

"And now the question comes," the old document goes on to recite, "who was the father of Nancy Hanks, Lincoln's mother?" Lucy Hanks, her mother, was never married to any Hanks, as far as I can find out, nor to any other person before or after she married Henry Sparrow, or before she had Nancy.

When Nancy Hanks was born, who was Lucy Hanks' husband? This is quite a pertinent question. What did Lincoln say to Scripps, his campaign biographer? No one need for this matter rely on what I say, or have said, that Lincoln told me his mother was "illegitimate." He told me his mother was an "illegitimate child of a Virginia Planter, or large farmer. However the record tells its own story, and speaks for itself; and had not the record spoken out, it is more than probable that I should have kept the "secret" forever, though I was not forbidden to reveal the fact after Lincoln's death. I never uttered this to mortal man directly or indirectly until after the death of Lincoln.

And now again, who was the father of Nancy Hanks, the mother of the President of the United States? Will some gentleman, some lady, kindly tell me? The father of Nancy Hanks is no other than "a Virginia Planter, large farmer, of the very highest and best blood of Virginia"; and it is just here that Nancy got her good, rich blood, tinged with genius. Mr. Lincoln told me that she was a genius, and that he got his mind from her.

Nancy Hanks Lincoln was a woman of very fine cast of mind, an excellent heart, quick in sympathy, a natural lady, a good neighbor, a firm friend. Good cheer and hilarity generally accompanied her; and had she been reared at all well, she must have flourished anywhere; but as it was. she was rude and rough, breaking and having difficulty, through all forms, conditions and customs, habits, etiquettes of society. She could not be held to forms and methods of things. And yet she was a fine woman, naturally.

It is quite probable that a knowledge of her origin had made her defiant and desperate. She was very sensitive, and sometimes gloomy. Who will tell me the amount and influence of her feelings in this matter, caused by her origin? Let the world forgive her, and bless her, is my constant prayer.

Lincoln often thought of committing suicide. Why? Did the knowledge of his mother's origin, or his own, press the thought of suicide upon him? Who will weigh the force of such an idea as illegitimacy on man or woman, especially when that man or woman is very sensitive, such as Lincoln was? God help such people (Barton, *Paternity*, pp. 50-54).

It may be that the "record" containing the "secret" in regard to the paternity of Nancy Hanks in the hands of the historian Herndon was a copy of the "record" written by Columbus Tanner containing the family "secret" held by the Tanner family. And this old "record" very strongly hints that Abraham Lincoln was an illegitimate, and that this fact furnished the foundation for all his "melancholia."

CHAPTER SEVEN

The Great American Sphinx

Having found a suitable intellectual background for Abraham Lincoln's mother, in the well-to-do family of Tanners of German descent, we will now offer to the reader what we conceive to be an adequate and satisfactory solution of one of the greatest riddles of all history.

Taking into consideration his surroundings, the barrenness and poverty of all his environment and influences, including Thomas Lincoln as the "father" of this boy of the "sad face," we have in Abraham Lincoln a Sphinx-like character which dares and stubbornly challenges every writer of American history and biography. His intellectual genius, his peculiar sympathies for the poor and unfortunate, his gluttonous appetite for reading and the study of "books," with his tall, angular body, offer a constant and incessant protest against the shamery and falsity of most of the history written of this man.

The American people detest "shamery" in any form and they would be glad to know the unvarnished truth about Lincoln's origin. They know he did not make himself nor was he an angel handed down from Heaven. And they are slow to believe that race horses can suddenly spring up from long-eared donkey; they don't much believe in the Darwinian theory, though this has often been offered as a proof text. Yet here stands the boy, the man, the President as a political Gibraltar, offering the only gateway to the freedom of an enslaved race.

If it is true that William E. Herndon, Lincoln's personal friend, partner in the law firm and first biographer of Lincoln, found upon close contact what he called "a skeleton and cancer" in Abraham Lincoln's origin, the people would like to know what it is. If your best friend should be sick, you, as a friend, would like to know what the trouble is.

Mr. Herndon, the historian, advised the following writers to "dig to the bottom" of some things that some writers contended should be suppressed and "consigned to the tomb" (Herndon and Weik). But Herndon said:

> Mr. Lincoln was my warm friend. I always loved him, and revere his memory to this day. My purpose to tell the truth about him need occasion no apprehension; for I know that God's naked truth, as Carlyle puts it, can never injure the fame of Abraham Lincoln.
>
> Some persons will doubtless object to the narrative of certain facts, which appear here for the first time, and which they contend should be consigned to the tomb. Their pretense is that no good can come from such ghastly exposures. To such over-sensitive souls, if any such exist, my reply is that these facts are indispensable to a full knowledge of Mr. Lincoln in all the walks of life (Herndon and Weik).

The "narrative" of these facts which were so objectionable to some people have been omitted from the second edition of Herndon's valuable work, but in the first edition he says:

> If the story of his life is truthfully and courageously told, nothing colored or suppressed, nothing false either written or suggested, the reader will see and feel the real presence of the man.
>
> If, on the other hand, the story is colored, or the facts in any degree suppressed, the reader will not only be misled, but imposed upon as well. At last the truth will come and no man

need hope to evade it (Introduction to Herndon's First Edition on Lincoln).

The statement is made in R. G. Horton's *Youth's History of the Great Civil War*, on the question of Lincoln's ancestry, that:

> He had the misfortune to not know who his father was; and his mother, alas, was a person to reflect no honor upon her own child. Launched into the world an outcast, and started on the road of being without parental care, and without the advantage of even a common school education, he certainly was entitled to great credit for gaining even the limited mental culture which he possessed.
>
> He ran away from his wretched home at the age of nine to escape the brutal treatment of the man who had married his mother, and was forced to get his bread by working on a flat-boat on the Mississippi.

We have the following in the *History of Lincoln* by W. H. Lamon, one of the earliest historians:

> At the time of his [Abraham Lincoln's] birth they were supposed to have been married about three years. Although there appears to have been little sympathy or affection between Thomas and Abraham Lincoln, they were nevertheless connected by ties and associations which make the previous history of Thomas Lincoln and his family a necessary part of any reasonably full biography of the great man who immortalized the name by wearing it.

It has been claimed by some critics that Lamon, the historian, strongly intimated in the above paragraph that Abraham Lincoln was minus a legal father, and that upon this account his historical work has largely been "suppressed."

Violence to the Basic Principles of Historical Research

In the face of all the early statements, the apologizing historians have written voluminously in their efforts to belittle and gloss over what the historians had to say about Abraham Lincoln's origin. Especially of note among this company of apologists is the late Dr. Barton, who carried with him a "spade" with which he proposed to bury all "such scandalous stories deep down close upon the confines of Hades" (Barton, *Paternity of Lincoln*).

But among the various efforts which Mr. Barton put forth to cover up the old traditions of the Lincoln ancestry, none appear so futile and of so little weight as criticism of the old document in William Herndon's handwriting, "written about 1866 to 1877."

This popular historian frequently does violence to the basic principles of historical research and criticism, in his book on *The Paternity of Abraham Lincoln* (pp. 38, 50, 51, 73, 74, 83, 84, 89, 115, 231, 306, 315-319, et al).

The student of Eugenics and Heredity will very quickly detect in this old writing called by Dr. Barton "a remarkable document," the very highest evidence of a very superior ancestry for Lincoln's mother. This is contradictory of the statement of President Woodrow Wilson, that Lincoln's parents were "trash." I suppose he believed, like some others who were not very well informed upon this question, that just a few long jumps of "evolution" could make a first-class President from intellects in a class with the "Jukses," a family that has cost the State of New York over two million and a half dollars. But such a miraculous feat has never been performed. All such jumps are only imaginary.

I offer an aphorism upon the truth of which I challenge all comers of the scientific world as follows: "All mind is from mind." And the same quality of mentality, as seed, produces its kind and no other. If it is of a low grade of intellect, it will always produce a low grade. It can not produce intellectual people from inferior mental seed. And the mind is not produced from brain cells but from primordial mental cells as seed. The mentality of people is inherited in the protoplasm, and not through brain organization (Coggins on *Mentality*).

Yes, as William Herndon says: "Lincoln's mother was of a very fine cast of mind, an excellent heart, quick in sympathy, a natural lady, a good neighbor, a firm friend." And when you go among the Tanners from North Carolina to New York you will find this same class of people,

The seed, true to the fundamental law of the cell, always produces its kind.

And it is nothing but common honesty and a square deal to tell the people the plain truth about this matter. Then, who was Abraham Lincoln's real father? Nancy Hanks, though sired by "the best blood of Virginia" could not produce him by herself! And it requires high intellect in both ancestors to produce an intellectual "genius." I think the late developments in science will bear testimony to this fact. And Nancy Hanks Tanner is mentally equipped to be his mother, but we must have just as good a sire for Lincoln's real father.

CHAPTER EIGHT

☆ ☆ ☆ ☆

The Enloe Family's Ancestry

The following is excerpted from the Hon. James H. Cathey's, *Truth is Stranger Than Fiction* (pp. 162-177):

> Three Enloe brothers, forbears of the family, landed about the middle of the 17th century in Maryland. They came from Scotland and England. One of these brothers settled on Lord Baltimore's land and reared a family. The other two went from Maryland to South Carolina and made their home in York district [I think they were Gilbert and Scroop].
>
> These old Enloes were school teachers by profession, men of liberal education. From these three men have sprung a numerous progeny, scattered over Maryland, Georgia, South Carolina, Tennessee, Kentucky, Illinois, Missouri, California, and Texas.
>
> It is remarkable the number of strong men throughout this long line. We fearlessly invite anyone who may feel skeptical as to this assertion to investigate for himself.
>
> All down the line from the day when the South Carolina grandsires began to "train the young idea to shoot," to the present when they sit in legislatures, in Congress, and upon the Bench, the Enloes have undoubtedly contributed materially to the building of the Republic.
>
> They have marched in the forefront of frontier settlement,

undaunted by the sternest difficulties.

They have introduced civil government in the wilderness, and modestly, yet liberally, contributed to the support of its institutions.

They have helped make, construe, and enforce the laws by which they have been governed.

Wherever duty called, in peace or war, they have cheerfully responded.

Wherever they have dwelt, they have distinguished themselves for intelligence, industry and probity.

Wherever they have planted themselves, thrifty farmers, successful merchants, physicians, jurists and legislators have sprung up.

Physically, they are rather large, tall, slender, but rawboned as a rule, and sinewy.

Mentally they are vigorous and alert, and all through the line, in an individual here and there, there is a vein of natural humor.

Abraham Enloe

One of the sons of an Enloe family at York, South Carolina, by the name of Abraham Enloe married a Miss Egerton and located in what is now Rutherford County, North Carolina. The records in the office of the Register of Deeds show that Abraham Enloe owned a dozen different farms in that County, besides the property he owned at other places. He also owned slaves to work on his farms; and the records show that he often paid for his purchases in gold. This was in the latter part of the 18th century.

The oldest newspaper of Rutherford County, *The Vindicator*, speaks of Abraham Enloe as "a wealthy land holder and surveyor." It is stated as will appear further on, that this man was a very superior man, both mentally and physically. His was a "very striking personality." He was considerably over six feet tall and weighed from 250 to 300 pounds, rawboned. His hair was black and coarse. He had deep-set grey eyes and dark skin. His mental tendency was toward the legal profession. He was a Magistrate, and tried a great many cases.

In all this Magistrate's trials, it was his custom to effect a compromise between the parties in litigation where it was at all possible, but when he saw that this could not be done, he became firm and unyielding for what he believed to be right (David Hyde).

This Abraham Enloe was also noted for his "charity" to the poor and unfortunate of his community. "No one who ever came to him for help day or night was ever turned away." He arose from his bed at midnight and went to his barn and got wheat for people who were out of bread. His family "wore silks and were called "stuck-ups" by some people of the community.

He was reared a "Scotch Presbyterian," and his home was the usual stopping place for the ministers of all faiths who chanced to come into his community. On the Lord's Day, Mr. Enloe would call his colored servants around him and read the Bible to them, often stopping to explain difficult passages of Scripture.

This man reared a family of sixteen children, nine boys and seven girls, and gave all of them a fairly good education for that day. And one very remarkable thing has been related in regard to his control of his family, especially the boys. It has been stated that "all nine of his sons remained with him till after they were twenty-one years old in perfect obedience to their father, not one ever raising his voice in disloyalty." This fact shows an unusual personality and strength of character, only very few people being able to wield such a strong influence over the older members of a family.

CHAPTER NINE

Nancy Hanks Enters the Enloe Home

Richard Hanks having miserably failed to provide the necessary comforts for the little family, including Nancy, it became imperative to place these children in better homes. And whether this happened when "Dick" was put in jail at Rutherfordton or immediately after he was burned to death we do not know.

But Nancy Hanks, the mother of President Lincoln, was, when a little girl, placed in the home of Abraham Enloe of Rutherford County, North Carolina. Some have said, "she was bound out" (B. H. Melton, et al). Here she worked as a member of the family and was taught with the other children to read and write; and she attended the Concord Baptist Church about a mile south of where Mr. Enloe lived on Puzzle Creek. Her girl friends attended this church and young Nancy Hanks went to church with them. And it is claimed by some of the old people that Nancy was a member of that church.

Here Nancy was happy; she could hear the Enloe Negroes sing in the fields of cotton and corn and she could listen to the sweet notes of the mocking birds and the brown thrush all 'round the big house on the hill. But there were moments when Nancy was not so happy as the birds, when she thought of the death of

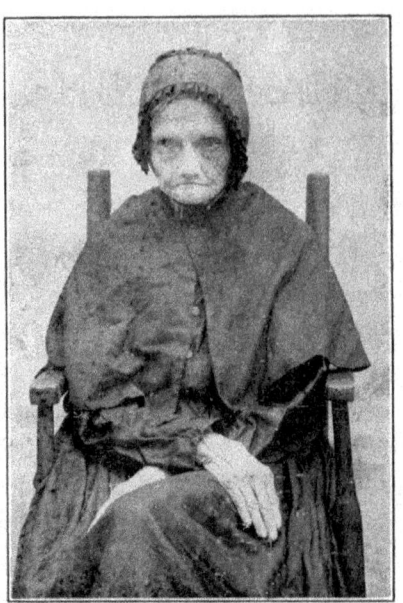

Nancy Hollifield, Age 107,
Playmate of Nancy Hanks

The above is a picture of one of Nancy Hanks' playmates, whose grandson, Mr. Brackston Smart, a farmer and Baptist minister, lives on the same farm and in part of the same house occupied by his grandmother a hundred and thirty years ago. This lady, when a girl, saw Nancy Hanks after little Abe was born at the old Enloe home, and was present to tell them "goodbye" when they left for Kentucky.

THE EUGENICS OF PRESIDENT ABRAHAM LINCOLN   93

her uncle "Dick" as she called him, and nobody to get him out of the fire until he was burned to a crisp. She often cried about his tragic end, and was consoled by Nancy Enloe, a fine girl about the same age of Nancy Hanks. These two girls were pals; they loved each other and were nearly always together.

But after a while, a young man who had been acquainted with the Enloes slipped in one night when Mr. Enloe was away from home and "stole" Nancy Enloe and took her off up the creek where they were married by the Baptist minister, Rev. Swabel. Of course Nancy Hanks went along and saw them married, after which they started for the young man Thompson's home in Kentucky, beyond the big mountains, and Nancy Hanks returned to Enloe's.

Among the outside girl friends whom Nancy Hanks made while she was an inmate of the Enloe home, were Polly Price and Nancy Hollifield. Polly lived on Duncan's Creek, and Nancy Hollifield lived about ten miles east of the Enloe home on Puzzle Creek. These two girls became devoted to the girl who became Abraham Lincoln's mother. And we are furnishing a picture of Nancy Hollifield in this book as one of Nancy Hanks' friends who often spoke of having had the pleasure of "holding Nancy's baby in her arms." Both of these girl friends, when the severe trial came later on, proved their unwavering devotion and love for the "orphan Nancy," as she was sometimes called.

In those days the neighbors had their social gatherings, sometimes at dances in a neighbor's home and at "quiltings," "corn shuckings," and "log rollings." The old folks claim that the girl, Nancy Hanks, attended some of these home dances; that she went to Duncan's Creek, about ten miles north, and danced at the home of Polly Price and that she went to Nancy Hollifield's and danced at her home; and that these girls came to the Enloe home and danced there, with Nancy and her friends.

The old log building is still standing on Duncan's Creek, in which these quiltings and dances were held when Lincoln's mother was one of the girl participants. And the same is true of the Hollifield building. But the old Enloe house which stood till just a few years ago has been torn down, with only the stone basement remaining as a quiet reminder of the place where the "wealthy citizen and surveyor" lived, and of whom it was related in after years that the picture of Abraham Lincoln appearing in the campaign papers was a perfect picture of Abraham Enloe (Col. Albert Logan in the Rutherfordton, N.C. *Vindicator*).

CHAPTER TEN

The Enloes Move To The Mountains

By this time some "great discoveries" had been made west of the Blue Ridge Mountains, and a goodly number of people were becoming very much interested in the "mountain country," a section of the great Appalachian system of Eastern America. This wonderful country offered the daring pioneers strong inducements to follow the example of the intrepid Daniel Boone, who but a few years earlier had left North Carolina and fought his way on into the State of Kentucky, where he founded permanent settlements. Now there is a considerable drift to the mountains.

Already there were well-beaten "trails" reaching from the Eastern Seaboard through this mountain country, formerly made by the wild Indians; and these old Indian trails were used as the first roads of the early White settlers. And it was not unusual for the White people to employ friendly Indians to pilot them over the "Great Smokies," a trip not entirely free from danger. And usually a number of families would make this trip together.

Abraham Enloe, "prominent and wealthy citizen of Rutherford County," decided, with three or four other neighbors of his community, to move to the mountains. These people who accompanied the Enloe family were the Hon. Felix Walker of

Abraham Lincoln's Mother in the Ox-Wagon

Abraham Lincoln's mother in the ox-wagon caravan, passing up through the great Chimney Rock Gorge, following an old Indian trail with the other members of the party.

"Speaking for Buncombe" fame in the Senate, and his family; John Plott and family, and a Mr. Battle; and probably a family by the name of Kennedy. The trip was made in ox-wagons, and Abraham Enloe had the only horses taken across the mountains at this time. They went up through the wonderful "Chimney Rock Gorge," crossing the mountain at "Hickory Nut Gap," and made their way through this beautiful wilderness to a section now in Jackson County called "Soco" by the Indians, not far from the present site of Bryson City, North Carolina.

Here the company was halted by a large company of wild Indians armed with their bows and arrows and ready for battle with the Whites. But the White people had not gone there for trouble. Though they had their guns and some large English mastiff dogs along, yet they were not able to meet such a formidable foe in such numbers at this time. This was an occasion demanding exceedingly fine diplomacy, and Abraham Enloe as the leading spirit of the party engaged the Indian chief and some of his leading warriors in a parley lasting for some time. Finally the Indians were led to believe these people meant to do them no injury and they became good friends. And it is claimed this friendship was never broken by either side.

Here the ox-wagon caravan came to an end, and the different members of the little party selected for themselves home sites. And Abraham Enloe marked off one square mile at the confluence of Soco Creek and the beautiful Ocona Lufta River, where he immediately built a large log house, the foundation of which is yet standing, and the land is yet held by his descendants. This is now known as one of the finest farms in Jackson County. This writer was the Principal of the high school there a few years ago and secured much valuable information from the old citizens and some old Indians of that community whose parents had known the Enloes well.

But, notwithstanding Mr. Enloe owned a dozen farms back in Rutherford County, and this "square mile farm on Soco," he was not satisfied. He soon found another location which pleased him better, a few miles farther up the river. And up at the confluence of "Raven's Ford" with the Ocona, he found just what he wanted. Here he secured two thousand acres, the real beauty spot of the mountain country, and built here his permanent mountain home. This was truly a mountain Paradise of indescribable beauty. Here were silvery waters clear as crystal, filled with the finest fish in the world, the speckled trout, and plenty of game of different kinds, and smooth, fertile river bottom land of several hundred acres surrounded by picturesque mountains enveloped in the rich emerald of spruce, with great natural gardens of rhododendron, Kalmia and honeysuckles. Truly, human eyes never beheld an earthly scene of more exquisite natural beauty than this, the last home of Abraham Enloe. Here with slave labor he cleared the land and cultivated his crops and passed the remainder of his days. And here he was buried.

As some indication to the reader as an adequate appraisal of this particular home site of Mr. Enloe, we will say that just half of this land was recently sold to the Government by the Floid brothers, grandsons of Enloe, to be a part of the National Park, for the sum of $80,000.00.

While we have dealt with Abraham Enloe and his various activities at considerable length, it is not without a good reason, as will be observed by the reader.

Nancy Hanks, Lincoln's mother, who had entered the Enloe home some years before, went with this Enloe family, and for a while made her home at this enchanted place in the mountains. She was now a young woman, between 18 and 20 years old.

CHAPTER ELEVEN

Nancy Hanks Is Driven From Home

It is related upon the very highest authority and from different sources that this girl of fine German ancestry was forced to leave the home of the Enloes. She was driven out of this Garden of Eden, not with a "flaming sword" but with a still hotter sword, the lashing and cutting tongue of Abraham Enloe's wife who claimed the social laws of this lovely place had been infringed; that forbidden fruit had been partaken of stealthily, and that as a result her (Mrs. Enloe's) private, personal and domestic happiness had been ruined forever! She talked it, she made no secret of what she knew; she told everybody who came that way about what trouble that girl, "the low-down Hanks girl," had given her since they had moved to the mountains. This occurred in about 1803 or 1804 as indicated in old records in Rutherford County (also see records at Asheville). Mrs. Enloe in very forceful language laid down the law to Nancy. "She told her to "pack up her duds and leave there and never come back!" And it is related upon good authority that Abraham Enloe also received his share of his angry wife's blessing. She told him that he was a very depraved piece of humanity, and that he had violated every vestige of his conjugal fidelity to her (Squire Potts, Wells, et al).

But Abraham does not intend to send this "Hagar" out to a wilderness to die. He has lived such a life among his neighbors that he has friends everywhere. The people "all look up to him and respect him," is the splendid record written by a neighbor, Phillip Dills. Enloe hurriedly sent word to his friend, the Hon. Felix Walker, who lived on Johnathan's Creek a few miles from Waynesville, to come to his (Enloe's) home just as soon as possible. Walker dropped everything and hurriedly rode across the Soco Gap to where Enloe lived on Ocona. Nancy was glad to leave, now that this Eden had become her Gethsemane.

Mr. Walker took the sorrowing girl back home with him, where she was offered a place to stay. But this was too near to the Enloe's. And Abraham Enloe had Mr. Walker go back to Rutherford County in search of a temporary home for Nancy Hanks among "her people." On this trip in search for a suitable place, he went to a member of the Tanner family, as it was thought she was close akin, a cousin to Dan Tanner's children.

But when they learned the circumstances, they refused to give her any "room in the inn." And when no place could be found among her own people, Felix Walker went to the former home of Abraham Enloe, on Puzzle Creek, to see the tenants who were renting this Enloe place, to see if they would take Nancy and provide her a comfortable home for a while.

These people were willing to give this poor Hagar, the outcast girl, homeless, motherless and fatherless, a place to stay. In her dark hours as she waited for the return of Walker, she had very strange dreams. She could see the old Enloe place and could hear the darkies singing in the cotton fields; she again joined with her girl friends, Polly Price and Nancy Hollifield, and ran down to the creek and waded upon its sandy bottom near the watermelon patch; in her dream they romped over and around the beautiful hill gathering wild flowers and in the midst of her glee she heard the bass noise of thunder and beheld a dark cloud quickly gathering. Immediately the hill was covered with people, and she found herself standing in the midst of the people beside a great golden altar with her arms full of sweet wild flowers, and these flowers, all that she had, she laid upon that golden altar.

When the girl awoke, Mr. Walker had returned and was ready to transport her back to the old home where she had spent many pleasant days and years in Rutherford County.

This Hagar soon saw the same old place, the same girl friends, and indeed, she saw a dark cloud coming, too! And one bright morning when her former companions called to see her, they found her with a fine, long-armed baby boy, whom she had already named Abraham! She had named him for his father. And this child was to be her gift to the multitudes upon the great golden altar!

The True Birth-Place of Abraham Lincoln,
One Mile North of Bostic, North Carolina

Only a pile of stones now marks the site of the first home of Abraham Enloe where Nancy Hanks was sent before her child was born. These stones were part of the basement where the baby was hidden when "unwelcome" visitors came.

CHAPTER TWELVE

Nancy Prepares To Go To Kentucky With "Little Abe"

About this time, a very startling and dangerous rumor had been started and circulated back in the mountains by someone not intimately informed upon this unpleasant situation.

While Abraham Enloe, in a quiet and diplomatic way, was busy doing everything he could for this girl, somebody had circulated the report that Enloe had "killed Nancy"! And of course one can easily see how such news can spread with some thing added by each one who relates the unpleasant story. And to add plausibility to the story, it was really a fact that Mr. Enloe had, himself, been "gone from his home about three weeks, and no one knew where he was." It was claimed that Nancy could not be found anywhere. Of course what had been done for her had been kept a secret. But the situation in the Enloe community is by this time getting ugly, and is frightfully dangerous to Mr. Enloe.

The entire community was stirred to the point where someone, who may have been peeved over the decision in a trial, as often happens, had suggested that Enloe be "lynched"! Abraham Enloe now makes another important move upon this checkerboard. He has a daughter in the State of Kentucky who had married a Mr. Thompson; and Enloe informs his married daughter about the unpleasant situation at his home, and asked her co-operation in straightening out the tangle.

This Mr. and Mrs. Thompson freely offered their services, even to the point of furnishing a new home for Nancy and little Abraham. They offered to come after the girl and take her back with them to Kentucky.

This good news was immediately dispatched to the poor girl, now down in Rutherford County, requesting that she prepare immediately for the trip to Kentucky. She was to come by way of Enloe's to save him from the threatened mob violence of the people who believed he had killed her (Story by A. DeK. Wallace; also by Edmond Davis Dill). It is remarkable how fast news of this kind can spread.

The Tanner family had been talking about the "trouble Nancy Hanks was in," and that she had wanted to come and stay with them; and they felt it their "duty" to let their "uncle Michael" know about it, maybe he could lend some assistance to his daughter in her "predicament," they said. Michael Tanner was probably then in Virginia.

So it happened that Michael learned of the situation just about the time Nancy received word to prepare to go to Kentucky.

Just at this time a "revival meeting" was going on at the Concord Baptist Church, of which Nancy was a member, it is claimed. And Nancy went to this meeting, taking her little Abraham along, to say goodbye to all her friends of the community, for she had no idea of ever seeing them again on earth, and Nancy loved these folks and they loved her with a genuine love, one that lasts when all the sham friendships are gone forever!

Here at the church Nancy felt very happy. The good sermon not only had the effect of making her feel remorseful and very penitent for all her misdeeds in life, but through her penitent tears and the earnest prayers of the good people a new hope was born in her sorrowing soul; a Heavenly "hope," which is "the Anchor to the Soul, both sure and steadfast, and entereth into that within the Veil" (Heb. 6:19).

Here were imparted the farewell kisses by the loving friends, and little Abraham was not omitted, for upon good authority it is related that Nancy's girl friends, Polly Price and Nancy Hollifield, took this baby in their arms and kissed him goodbye (George DePriest).

Nancy, having made the necessary preparation to take her expected departure for Kentucky, was only waiting now for the means of transportation which she hoped was on the way from Enloe's. This man had never failed her, and she hourly looked for the horseman.

The next morning after Nancy had attended the Baptist meeting, there appeared to be a new joy in her soul; a joy that involuntarily expressed itself in one of her favorite songs, "Jesus, Lover of My Soul." And while walking the floor with little Abraham hugged close in her arms, singing this great old hymn, she looked out at the window and saw a strange man coming, riding a fine large grey horse up the hill, He was not of that community she knew; he was a superior looking man. He rode like an Army officer, and was accoutered splendidly, as a man of wealth. She could not possibly divine who this stranger could be. Hitching his very splendid mount to a pine tree outside the yard fence this gentleman walked up the stone steps and rapped at the door. Nancy had gone back into the next room and asked the lady with whom she was staying to meet the gentleman at the door.

He told the lady of the house that he had been informed that there was a girl there by the name of "Nancy Hanks," and that he had come a long way to see her. And when Nancy came to the door he asked if she were the daughter of Lucy Hanks, and if she were the same girl who lived down on the Catawba River for a while, in the home of "Dick" (Richard) Hanks. Nancy saw that he was moved to tears by a deep emotion. And then he told her that his name was Michael Tanner, her father!

His people, the Tanners, had informed him that she was in very great trouble, and he had come to see if there was anything he could do to render her assistance. Then Nancy told Mr. Tanner, her father, the full story of her trouble. He was quick to detect in

A Paul Revere Ride

It was a Kentuckian who had met and fallen in love with a beautiful daughter of Abraham Enloe named Nancy, contrary to the father's wishes; but love found a way, and it was the Indian Trail and a ride by night on as swift a horse as Thompson could find. And later this same trail was followed by little Abraham and his mother as they went to Kentucky with this "runaway couple." And it was a son of this couple who was appointed by President Lincoln in 1861 as the disbursement agent for the Cherokee Indians, and this man who was appointed was a Democrat. These people had furnished a home for the homeless Nancy and her child who became the President.

her "sparkling grey eyes and high forehead and dark hair" an exact replica of the Tanner family! In this, his own mirror, Michael Tanner could see himself perfectly. No painter could paint a more perfect picture of her noble German ancestry.

Michael Tanner, "horse trader, mule drover, large planter of the best blood of Virginia," the father of Nancy Hanks, brought this girl back to Abraham Enloe (George DePriest and Atty. Riding).

We are not able to follow Michael Tanner any farther on this journey with his daughter and her babe than to the mountain country. There are two separate and distinct traditions: one that Nancy was taken to Kentucky by a "horse trader," Michael Tanner, and the other that she was taken there by the Hon. Felix Walker. But it is unlikely that both these gentlemen went with Nancy to Kentucky.

The story that the girl mother was taken to Kentucky by Mr. Walker was doubtless based upon the fact that someone saw Mr. Walker taking the girl away from Enloe's, and as it was later reported that she had gone to that State, they supposed that she had been taken directly there by Walker.

The fact is, it was not necessary for either of these gentlemen to make the trip to Kentucky unless they especially wanted to go, for the arrangements had already been made for this journey by Abraham Enloe.

The Thompsons were already at Enloe's, waiting for Nancy; and they had secured the services of a trusted Indian guide to go back with the party across the Great Smokey Mountains (A Miss Davidson and Styles, attorney of Asheville, N.C.; Barton's *Paternity of Lincoln*, p. 203; Arthur's *History of Western North Carolina*, pp. 308- 326).

There is a very striking and peculiar corroboration of this incident on file in Washington City, in Abraham Lincoln's files of his appointments. How long Nancy and little Abraham remained at the home of the Thompsons we do not know, but there is a story that when Lincoln was President he made a trip to see his half-sister, Mrs. Thompson, who years before had given a home to him and his homeless mother; he asked if there was anything he could do for her and she replied that he could do nothing for her, but if he wished he might do something for her son who was about the age of Lincoln, and President Lincoln appointed this Thompson as the head of the Department for Disbursements for the Indians. This Thompson was a Democrat, yet he held this office while Lincoln lived, and it is claimed that Lincoln did the same for another Enloe relative (*Lincoln Records*, Washington, show appointment of this Thompson, March 26, 1861; Attorney Styles, each of whom held important positions during the Presidency of Abraham Lincoln).

CHAPTER THIRTEEN

Nancy Hanks' Kentucky Beau

This North Carolina "Hagar" has added one more to the long list of "Nancy Hankses" in the State of Kentucky, a late writer, Dr. Warren, claiming to have found more than twenty in that State. Hence in this wilderness of girls by the same name it behooves any scribe to proceed with caution, lest he might get them "mixed up," as were the Jersey calves in George Vanderbilt's dairy barn. One thing is sure, however, and that is that the friends of the North Carolina girl will not be interested in some other Nancy than this one reared in the family of Abraham Enloe; and the reader may look out for this contact. For such contact may furnish the positive proof, among so many, of this young woman's identification.

We are now very positive that the great majority of historians have so constructed the record as to make it appear to the reader that Thomas Lincoln courted and was married to the wrong Nancy Hanks, a pseudo "composite" character, who was not the wife of Tom Lincoln at all. They would have him court a Nancy who had no child as an embarrassing encumbrance; a Nancy two or three or four years too old; a Nancy with a "sensitive mouth, and kindly, gentle manner. Bright, scintillating, noted for her keen wit and repartee, who had withal a loving heart" (Mrs. Hitchcock, p. 51), a Nancy having the wrong father and the wrong mother, to be eligible to qualify for the mother of President Lincoln (Dr. Barton, *Paternity of Lincoln*, p. 272; Dr. Louis Warren, *Lincoln's Parentage and Childhood*, pp. 72, 73).

    This "beautiful" Hitchcock production will have to stand aside. She fails to fit the rigid requirements of this case. For President Lincoln himself turns her down as his mother, saying "his mother was the 'illegitimate' daughter of Lucy Hanks" and a "well-bred Virginia farmer, or large planter of the best blood of Virginia." This fits neither the father nor mother popularly portrayed as the mother of Lincoln. He would not have known her if he had met her in the road. He would have regarded her as a stranger, which she was, to him.

    Lincoln's unpainted, unmanufactured mother had "dark skin, dark hair, a high forehead, small grey or 'hazel' eyes, face sharp and angular, and was 'above the average in height, with a marked expression of melancholy which fixed itself in the memory of all who ever saw or knew her'" (Herndon, *Life of Lincoln*, Vol. I, pp. 13-14). And she was not so old as the painters have made her; for the Kentucky girls were not required by law to have someone sign their marriage "bonds" after they were over the age of twenty-one. But Nancy Hanks was required to get someone to sign for her; and the record is, that she had Richard Berry, her uncle, to sign her bond, thus proving she was not the Nancy who was 23 years old at this time, the "beautiful, scintillating" little blond!

    Then it happens, too, that there appears no other Kentucky beauty of this name to occupy this very important position; and this must be filled, for President Lincoln must have a mother. He must have an unpainted mother whom he can recognize when he meets her.

    When Lucy Hanks, Nancy's mother, married Henry Sparrow in Kentucky, she signed her own bond for her marriage in 1790; and while Dr. Warren claims that the word "widow" very significantly appears above her name, I contend this was only a piece of camouflage to cover an unfavorable record, as people knew she had at least two children, though she had not been married (Herndon's "record").

Thomas Lincoln Was Hired to Marry Nancy

Then it was the North Carolina "Hagar" whom Thomas Lincoln courted, wooed and won. And this bright girl was "far superior to Tom Lincoln"; and had it not been for her encumbrance she never would have thought of having this "intellectually subnormal" for her husband. Every movement of Thomas was an indication of his inferiority to Nancy Hanks. She felt her superiority to this man whose only occupation at that time was the making of liquor. He was "born tired," and never could catch up with his rest. His uncle, Isaac Lincoln, drove him off from his place near Elizabethton, Tennessee, for his fondness for rest (J.D. Jenkins' letter).

And with all of Nancy's superior gifts, yet this "gallant" Kentucky suitor was not willing to marry her unless he could collect something from the father of Nancy's child. Tom figured that he could get some real cash out of this transaction, for this baby's North Carolina father had money, and much of it (Lamon, pp. 8, 9; William Herndon quoted from First Edition by Barton, p. 57).

There are at least three different and independent witnesses who lend testimony in support of this story, that Tom Lincoln was "hired by Abraham Enloe" to marry Nancy Hanks.

1. Berry Henderson Melton, my mother's uncle, who claimed that he personally knew Nancy Hanks, Lincoln's mother when she was a girl in the home of his uncle Abraham Enloe, and that his uncle was to pay Thomas Lincoln $500.00 and a wagon and team if Tom would marry the girl and provide a home for her boy, Abraham.

2. A similar story was related by the Kennedy family, near neighbors of Enloe, who claim they were at Enloe's after the marriage of Tom and Nancy, and saw Mr. Enloe pay Thomas Lincoln some money and a mare and a mule. And a corroboration of this

story is found in a letter from the Lincoln family by the name of Jenkins, saying that Nancy and Tom, with the little boy, went on horseback from Abraham Enloe's to see Tom's uncle Isaac at Elizabethton, Tennessee. And another one corroborating these, relates that Thomas and Nancy Hanks stopped at Rutledge, near Knoxville, Tennessee, on their way from Isaac Lincoln's to Kentucky, where Nancy, Tom's wife, was employed as a cook for a "boarding house" (Joseph Pemberton, Knoxville). These stories fail to articulate with any other theory imaginable.

3. Then these, backed by the same stories in Kentucky, render this position irrefutable for these could not have been started without collusion and fraud, unless they had been true.

Yes, Thomas Lincoln was "hired," as related by both historians, Lamon and Wm. Herndon, to marry this girl. And this fact is the only solution for what some of the historians call a "mystery," as to where Thomas Lincoln found so much money at one time with which he could "buy a fine farm of 300 acres, making a substantial payment in cash!" (Dr. Warren, p. 54).

This very peculiar situation tallies exactly with the embarrassed situation Nancy Hanks was then in, and also with the fact that the father of her child had money and could pay the husband, whoever might marry her. And it is inconceivable that a man like Mr. Enloe would pay out money to support Tom Lincoln's boy.

This marriage may have been held up for some time, while Mr. Lincoln was trying to make this arrangement, for Enloe was then living like a king on his beautiful mountain estate in Jackson County, North Carolina.

Another strange puzzle to the popular historians is the peculiar fact that Nancy Hanks, daughter of Lucy Hanks, never lived with her mother in Kentucky; and had she been reared there as claimed she, very probably, would have made that place her home, and the name of Lucy Hankes' (Sparrow) husband would appear on Nancy's marriage bond; instead of the name of her uncle Berry.

That beautiful little "scintillating" blond has never been seen or heard of any more since Thomas Lincoln and Nancy Hanks were married, and it has been thought by some that she was "composed" just for that occasion. Anyway, Thomas Lincoln took the girl home with him, who had a little boy when she was married, for an old story was passed about at that time and soon after, by the people who were present at the wedding, that "Nancy's boy sat between Tom and Nancy as they rode home in the wagon." And in this same county there was a very persistent story that "the old people said that Nancy's child, called Abraham, was known to be in that county before she and Tom were married." All of this verifies the preacher's story as sworn to by Chief Justice Peters of the State of Kentucky.

Meeting Wild Indians

The party of emigrants met the wild Indians on Soco Creek in what is now Jackson County, north of Bryson City. The party of Whites were in great danger, and it required great tact and diplomacy to be able to handle this situation. But Abraham Enloe, a man of superior tact and intelligence, talked with the old Chief and others for some time and persuaded them that the Whites were not their enemies. Terms of peace were agreed upon that never were broken by either side. The descendants of these same Indians now have a great school there at Cherokee, supported by the Government.

CHAPTER FOURTEEN

The Wedding – Little Abe a Guest

Nancy Hanks and Thomas Lincoln were married June 12, 1806, by the Rev. Jesse Head, a Methodist preacher. And there has never been another wedding this side of Adam and Eve that has been the subject of so much discussion, doubt and speculation. And all this discussion, reaching from the "snuff-box and brush" addicts on to historians, Congressmen and Presidents, was caused by Nancy's innocent little Abraham. And he could not help it if he did happen to be present at his mother's wedding.

There have been tons and tons of good paper wasted, trying to prove that this child was not yet born; and they can just as easily prove the absence of his mother as they can his own, from this wedding. And some think they have fully established an alibi for both of these people, from North Carolina. And yet they have shown the absence of that "beautiful" blond; for Tom Lincoln would not have known her himself. She was a stranger to Thomas Lincoln, as she doubtless was to everybody else (Dr. Warren, pp. 72-73).

Now, if we discard both of these girls, we will have left Thomas Lincoln without any wife! And there would be no use of trying to write any more history about Lincoln. For he himself would become a myth, without a mother.

But we can show, upon the very highest evidence that Abraham Lincoln (Enloe) was present, and that he followed wherever the family moved, from that time on.

The old story which was written up in the Mount Sterling, Kentucky newspaper by Judge Belvard January Peters, a Chief Justice of the Supreme Court of the State of Kentucky, is first-class testimony. The substance of this public press statement was later sworn to by the Hon. Judge Peters as having been based upon the statement of the minister who performed the marriage ceremony for Thomas Lincoln and Nancy Hanks.

This published statement was doubtless made by this judge while Abraham Lincoln was yet living. It may have been during the political campaign in which Lincoln engaged in 1860, that this appeared in the papers. For the same kind of story was published in 1861, in Tennessee, carrying an article saying "Lincoln, the President, was born in North Carolina, that his father's name was Enloe, and that he lived in Western North Carolina."

These press reports were in perfect keeping with the political temperature of the time, and were in answer to questions propounded in the newspapers of that campaign, asking, "Who is this man, Lincoln?" And the reply in one paper was, "We don't know; all we know is that he is the son of Nancy Hanks!" (Illinois paper – Mrs. Keeder in this book).

It seems that if Dr. Barton had been as interested in this as he was in trying to "bury" all such reports, he might have gotten the date of the Mount Sterling publication. At any rate, it is altogether improbable that Judge Peters published this after the death of Abraham Lincoln.

Now this judge was no fool; he knew the law upon such matters as libel and slander, and he was not the kind of man to put his head into that kind of trap, if these things were not true then not in his possession!

Sometimes an editor goes off half-cocked, and is sued for big damages, but Judge Peters was not sued, and all was quiet then, for there was no one who could dispute his statements – he published in his paper the real, unvarnished truth.

Why did not Abraham Lincoln answer these published reports? His law partner, Herndon, says: "Lincoln was constantly getting such messages" during the campaign, but "he never answered one of them." As a good lawyer, Lincoln knew that in the eyes and implication of the law, his perfect silence would be accepted as his acknowledgment of the truthfulness of these reports. Lincoln, thus, acknowledged his illegitimacy.

We know the law upon such matters. And we are quite sure that Lincoln would not have remained "silent" had not these reports been true.

He could have accumulated quite a fortune in a little while from such damage suits. And Abraham Lincoln was no ostrich, who in the face of an enemy or evil report, instead of putting up an honorable defense, would hide his face in the sand! Let the brainless think so if they wish; but Lincoln was utterly helpless; the stories were true!

Herndon says, "These stories became so common and scandalous, that Mr. Lincoln received only six votes from La Rue County, Kentucky, yet this County furnished 500 soldiers for the Union army" (Herndon; Barton, p. 129). There is no good reason for side-stepping or discrediting this outstanding statement of the historian, and friend of President Lincoln.

This "giant," who whipped three boys in a fist fight at Hogden's Mill, and threw the big bully, Jack Armstrong, and pinned him to the ground in the dust in the midst of a bunch of roughnecks, all against this young man Lincoln, now becomes profoundly dumb in the face of the reports about his "illegitimacy."

Why is Lincoln speechless, if these stories are false? Is he unable to defend his own or the family's honor? Why did not his law firm immediately file a suit for libel and slander? And it was his duty to do this. It is unthinkable that he placed such a low estimate upon his reputation as to consider any defense useless.

Elizabethtown Stories

And this same kind of story followed right on to where the Lincoln family lived at Elizabethtown, Kentucky. The residents of that town claim that they were acquainted with this little boy. And they further claim that an Abraham Enloe was his father! And instead of fitting an Enloe in Kentucky the description perfectly fits the North Carolina situation.

If Thomas Lincoln had left the Enloe "Hagar" out of consideration, what a lot of trouble and confusion it would have saved! Then he would not have had to move about so much to keep away from these stories about him being "hired to marry his wife." Then they would not have been put to the impossible task of trying to prove that Nancy's boy was several years younger than himself. Or that Nancy and Abraham Enloe's boy was younger than Tom and Nancy's girl, born at Elizabethtown, Kentucky. And he would not have had to engage in that "Bulldog fight with the North Carolina Enloe, for beating up Nancy and little Abe" so unmercifully, and the name of Tom's second child, little Thomas, who had to be left out of the family record to prevent a head end collision with Enloe's boy, could have been recorded as having been born at his own correct time and place, at Hodgensville (Dr. C. C. Graham's affidavit). And it would have saved the country from the big "snow storm" that Dennis Hanks started, in which a youth by the name of "Abraham Enloe" was blown over to Tom Lincoln's little log cabin on a cold night and found a "little boy baby in bed with Tom's wife." And it would have helped to avert the present great depression by saving the great material and expense of printing over a thousand different large books written to try to prove to people that first class game chickens can be raised from buzzards, upon the principle of "evolution"!

But, if Thomas had married the little blond "beauty" whom he perhaps didn't know, or didn't have a chance to marry, he would have made it so much easier for the historians. It would have saved them endless embarrassment. If they wanted to write the truth, they could not do it; for people wanted it the other way. They were mad over the earliest printed reports, and clamored like the mob before the Court of Pontius Pilate. And it is honestly thought that tons of printed material was destroyed because it was censored as socially and politically unfit for the public to read! And some who, left alone, having made up their minds to tell the people the "naked truth" as one put it, finally desisted (Barton p. 310).

The Wrong Enloe in the Elizabethtown Story

Dr. Barton and other apologists have concentrated all their navies, submarines, land, sea and air forces, and nearly all is hot air, on an innocent man in this case. This is a good man in Kentucky by the same name as the North Carolina Enloe, "Abraham." And it is just as necessary to be able to distinguish these different Enloes as it is to be able to distinguish different Nancy Hankses. Both the Nancy's could not be the mother of Abraham Lincoln; and both these Abraham Enloes can not possibly be the father of "Abraham Lincoln."

But it has frequently happened that a story, good or bad, has been inadvertently applied to the wrong person of two or more of the same name, and so it was in the case of the Kentucky Enloe, upon whom uninformed and unguarded writers have unloaded so much ammunition to no purpose.

"Yes sir, we all like Abe Lincoln down here, and it is no fault of his that Abe Enloe got mixed up with the hired girl and paid Tom Lincoln to marry her and move over to Hodgenville." (A bus driver at Elizabethtown reported in Barton, pp. 186, 187).

But this was spoken by a citizen of Elizabethtown about a former resident of that town by the name of Abraham Enloe. And the critics just riddled this story. They held it up to scorn and contempt as a piece of absolute fabrication; and showed that "this Abraham Enloe was not old enough to be the father of Abraham Lincoln at this time and that Nancy, the mother of Lincoln, never lived in that Enloe's home as a "hired girl," and, moreover, that

Tom Whipped Both Nancy and Little Abe

After Tom Lincoln married Nancy he became jealous of Enloe, who, hearing of her distress, sent her as much as fifty dollars at a time. And Tom would take his spite out in whipping the little boy and Nancy interfered and he whipped her till the blood ran down to her shoes. He was very brutal in his treatment of this child.

this Enloe and the Lincoln's were always upon good terms, and had never engaged in any 'fight'" (Barton, et al).

But because only one factor or one element of a story is untrue does not legally destroy all of the other parts. This story could all be based upon facts by supplying another Abraham Enloe, the one living in North Carolina, and in whose home Lincoln's mother did formerly live.

And the reader will not fail to note this corroboration in these separate and independent stories notwithstanding the minor variations. One will hardly ever hear two or more witnesses relate the same incident in exactly the same way. In fact, it makes the case stronger, for the witnesses to present the matter from different angles, when there is a correlation of the basic facts as in this case. The different stories furnish the very strongest evidence that there is some substantial foundation for their currency in different States.

Now I call the reader's attention to our former suggestion: "to look out for some contact between some friends in North Carolina with Tom and his wife if he married the girl who lived at Enloe's." The North Carolina people will not be especially interested in the folks in the State of Kentucky whom they do not know.

It has been a bit condoned, but not positively denied, that Thomas Lincoln did "treat little Abraham with great brutality," as related by Tom's own son-in-law, Col. Chapman. And if this were true, such barbaric treatment would be highly resented, and especially by the man who was the actual father of this child if he should learn about such conduct. And more especially would such be the case in the event that the real sire had already paid out some money for the maintenance of the child.

At that time, it was much more difficult to keep such transactions a secret, as the sending of large sums of money from one State to people in another State. And that Tom Lincoln had married the North Carolina Nancy Hanks is now positively proven by the fact that the North Carolina people are especially interested in this girl.

Nancy, Tom's Wife, Receives Money

It was a current rumor that Nancy had married a "very poor man, who was a very poor stick," and that there was no floor in her cabin; that she had no good beds and but little to eat. And it is related that this news reached the ears of Abraham Enloe of Ocona Lufta, North Carolina.

The reaction to this kind of a report of Nancy's unpleasant situation is just what might be expected under similar circumstances. There is no one on earth who would be so likely to lend this woman financial aid in her poverty and distress as the father of her first-born child, Abraham Enloe. And the girl's sad situation reached Enloe's heart and pocket-book as well as his ears. And my mother's uncle told me that his "uncle Abraham sent her as much as $50.00 at one time, and that Tom Lincoln got drunk and whipped little Abe so brutally that Nancy interfered and tried to stop him, and Tom turned upon her and beat her till the blood ran down to her shoes"! (B.H. Melton)

News of this "brutality" was carried to Enloe in North Carolina, and he went to Kentucky to investigate this matter. He found a very bad situation, and then the pent-up fires burst forth in that terrific battle between these two men in which Enloe's nose was bitten, and Enloe refused to pay Tom the full amount of "$500.00 and the wagon and the team." But after making friends, they compromised by Enloe paying a part of the money and a mare and a mule (B.H. Melton, Enloe's nephew; Rev. Kennedy).

Historians have imagined that there was some "underground" source from which Tom Lincoln could pick up money, when it did not appear that he had been working to make any money, and here is the sequel.

The questions as to who Lincoln was, during his campaign, revived all these unpleasant reminiscences; and then this story about the great fight between Abraham Enloe and Thomas Lincoln was published in *Bledsoe's Review*, and from there it went into the first two histories of Lincoln by Herndon, and also by Lamon.

But since the late historians are not able to find any record

Little Abraham's Father Fights Tom Lincoln

Abraham Enloe heard about Tom's brutality and went to see if it were really true; and he engaged old Tom in a terrible fight for whipping Nancy and the child so brutally; and in this fight the old turtle bit Enloe's nose. But they made friends, and Tom brought Nancy and the little boy over the mountains to see the Enloes. And Mr. Enloe gave Tom a mare and a mule and some money, as had formerly been promised.

or cause of such fight between Tom Lincoln and the boy called "Abraham Enloe," son of Esom Enloe, in Kentucky, they declare "there never was any such fight." They have just about deprived Lincoln of any mother, and soon they will claim that he is another "Melchizedek."

"Lincoln In His Shirttail"

One of the most peculiar things happened in the little town called Elizabethtown, Kentucky, just after Thomas and Nancy located there, soon after their marriage.

Of course it was often necessary for Mrs. Tom Lincoln to make trips to the store, and her little boy would naturally want to go along. And it was not long till the town folks were all well acquainted with the Lincoln family. At that time, little Abe would toddle along holding his mother's hand; and the people became very well acquainted with the situation. They had heard that this little fellow was not Tom's son, but was the son of Abraham Enloe, and that he was born at some other place than in that part of Kentucky.

Presley Haycraft, in his *History of Elizabethtown, Kentucky,* says he knew little Abraham Lincoln there at Elizabethtown, as a "little boy in his shirttail, holding to his mother's apron or hand."

And John B. Helm, who kept the store at that time, also remembered this little fellow. After becoming a judge, this man Helm told people and also told Abraham Lincoln that he knew him when he was little at Elizabethtown, and that he often fed him (Lincoln) on brown sugar. And Abraham Lincoln replied that he also remembered eating that sugar! Of course this is something a boy will not soon forget.

But now the inexplicable thing about this story is that, although both this storekeeper and Abraham Lincoln remember this incident very well, corroborating the historian, Mr. Haycraft's statement that he knew little Abe, having often seen him there in his little shirttail, yet these late high-brow apologists dig up the buried chronological tablets and to their consternation they find that "Abraham Lincoln was not yet born, if his correct birthday is on February 12, 1809"! Yet he ate that sugar two years before the year 1809. Now they say something has to be done about this glaring discrepancy, for a babe is not able to eat sugar that long before its birth.

And it is highly pertinent at this point to state that Thomas Lincoln's tax list for the year that he lived in Elizabethtown is complete, except the part of the page upon which was listed the names of the children in his family! Certainly this may have just happened, and ordinarily would not carry any suspicion, but under the peculiar circumstances it does carry considerable weight in this case. For little Abraham would appear upon this page if it had not been torn out! And this would have shown that he was born before Thomas and Nancy were married in 1806. So this important page and also the record of Thomas, Jr. are both missing.

Mr. Colin, the County Attorney, claimed that the aggregate of names on the tax lists indicated that the list belonged to the year 1809, but for some reason this page had disappeared. And there had also been some evidence that a younger son, by the name of Thomas, had been born at Hodgensville; and if so this was the child at whose birth the old people were present, who thought they had witnessed the birth of the President.

And we are informed that Mr. C. E. Howard, who now owns the original log cabin occupied by the Lincoln family at Knob Creek, has in his possession the headstone of a little grave on the top of the hill near by, and on this stone are the initials, "T.L." This is the very strongest corroborative evidence of our position, that little Thomas Lincoln was the child born at Hodgensville in 1809.

CHAPTER FIFTEEN

Historical Vandalism

It will appear from what has been brought out, and from what will yet follow, that there has been a persistent and unjustified destruction of very important historical matter, and especially is this true in regard to the history of Abraham Lincoln's childhood.

As all great men have their periods of childhood, the same as ordinary people, it is expected that Mr. Lincoln was not an exception to the rule. But it appears to some of the historians that Lincoln was lacking in this respect. He had no childhood whatever if people are to believe the majority of the historians. Thus writes Dr. Louis Austin Warren in his book *Lincoln's Parentage and Childhood* (page 140). This writer says:

> Those who have attempted to tell the story of Lincoln's childhood in Kentucky have usually made him a youth rather than a child. They have related incidents that no boy in early childhood could experience. There is no reason to believe that Abraham Lincoln was other than a normal child. Before reaching the age of eight years there would be no opportunity for that phenomenal growth which sometimes takes place in the early years of adolescence. We can not think of any peculiar mental gifts that set him

apart from his associates as a genius, and he was certainly too young to demonstrate any marked moral trait or any disposition toward morbidness.

When we remember that Abraham Lincoln moved to Indiana with his parents as he was approaching his eighth birthday, we shall not expect directly to learn very much about him during these childhood days.

Now let us assist Dr. Warren in the analysis of this peculiar "childhood" period in the life of Abraham Lincoln. This historian must grant or concede that Lincoln and his early Kentucky playmates were capable of remembering the early incidents and outstanding experiences of their own childhood better than present historians.

It certainly is not the part of a historian to manufacture a childhood for Abraham Lincoln, filling in this vacuum with an orchard of fine "cherry trees" all in bloom. Why not permit the old people who knew Lincoln and Mr. Lincoln himself to have their say about those early days in Kentucky? That is the only reasonable thing to do, as a historian. Then adjust the chronology to fit the actual life – instead of putting the boy into a mill and chopping him off and squeezing him up into a very much smaller person just to suit a fictitious date! If this old sham date, 1809, does not coincide with the early life of Lincoln, the historian to be true to his sacred mission, should change the date instead of changing the life-history of Abraham Lincoln, as related by people of the highest character, who knew they were telling the absolute truth and had no reason or occasion to falsify.

And especially should this procedure be followed by all historians, when there is perfect harmony, correlation, and corroboration in all these early stories of Mr. Lincoln's boyhood in Kentucky. If these old people were all liars, there would be a very marked lack of correlation among themselves. And they would constitute an "Ananias organization" of no small size. But why should they thus conspire without any reason to defeat the truth and manufacture a history to suit themselves? Did these old Kentucky people do this? No, they did not. Such is unthinkable! When all the circumstances, in connection with these early stories are considered together, the overwhelming weight of evidence will crush this fictitious date for Lincoln's birth, as a locomotive would crush a mole hill.

Stories of Abe's Early Childhood

Conspicuous among these early stories illustrating the "slaughter of the innocents," by late historians, is the one related by a prominent minister of Kentucky by the name of John Duncan. Rev. Duncan had written a letter to the first historian, Mr. Herndon, stating that he was born on July 5 1804. Herndon was writing a history of Lincoln and was getting all the information he could about the life of Lincoln. The letter was dated February 21, 1867, and Herndon's history gives this story as follows:

> John Duncan, afterwards a preacher of some prominence in Kentucky, relates how he and Abe on one occasion ran a ground hog into a crevice between two rocks and after working vainly almost two hours to get him out, Abe ran off about a quarter of a mile to a blacksmith shop and returned with an iron hook fastened to the end of a pole and with this rude contrivance they virtually "hooked" the animal out of his retreat.

Now, since it has been ascertained that the Duncans and the Lincoln's were neighbors on Nolin Creek, this brings these boys into contact. This innocent story has a good face and seems to be free from guile and deception. Yet it has been indicated as a piece of forgery or frame-up, as it contended that Lincoln was born in 1809 and could not have been old enough to hunt a ground hog.

But how easily this becomes possible in the light of the real truth, that this boy, Lincoln, was born before his mother went to the State of Kentucky, or ever saw Thomas Lincoln. So instead of being "only two years old" when this ground hog was caught, this boy was about seven or eight.

But let us see if these folks are liars: Here is another story, by another playmate of Lincoln, who fished young Lincoln out of Knob Creek. This is also related by the one, Austin Gallaher, who saved the life of Lincoln. This also has a good, honest face. The rescuer says, "On one occasion when attempting to 'coon' across the stream by swinging on a sycamore tree, Abraham lost his own hold and, tumbling into the deep water, was saved only by the utmost exertions of young Gallaher."

It seems that nearly all the dates as to the childhood activities of Abraham Lincoln have suffered the same fate as the record on that "lost" page of Tom's tax list. But, fortunately, this Knob Creek incident conveys a very valuable key to this whole Kentucky situation. In the first place, the young Gallaher and Abe were special friends, having gone to school together for more than a year when this happened. And this occurred, said Gallaher, in 1812. But according to popular chronology, Abe would have been only three years old (Lincoln gave his fish to a soldier of 1812, see Whipple, p. 9).

Now, it would be absurd to think that Abraham Lincoln had started to school when he was only two years old, walking two miles. But these boys did attend school together. And about a year before this a school had been started near Lincoln's home, so that if they were old enough they could attend this school together. And Austin Gallaher stated that they had attended school a year before this.

Evidently something is wrong. This incident, like catching the ground hog, fails to properly correlate with the manufactured date, 1809. But if 1809 should be correct as the year of this boy's birthday, and they "moved to Indiana in 1816," how could he get in his "three terms of school in Kentucky?" He would have been only seven when leaving the State.

Moreover, Gallaher tells, as preserved in a foot note in Nicolay and Hay (Vol. I, p. 27), that he was eleven years old and Lincoln was eight. Of course this may not have been exactly correct as to dates, yet the entire story is destroyed by holding on to 1809 as the true birthday of Lincoln. And it is highly probable that

Austin Gallaher told the truth when he said he and Lincoln "had been in school together a year or more."

Now if this Lincoln-Gallaher incident really took place in the year 1812, as Austin Gallaher related to the historian, then this boy did live with his folks at the town of Elizabethtown, and he did eat the sugar, and walked about with his mother as has been herein related. And he came to this town with his folks from the wedding, where he had been seen "running around on the floor," as sworn to as having been related by the preacher who married the couple.

For this would make little Abe about two years old when his mother was married in 1806. And this doesn't miss the real truth far. Then, this will give us the approximate time when Abraham (Enloe, Jr.) Lincoln, popularly known as Abraham Lincoln, was born back in North Carolina. "He was eight years old and had been going to school more than a year, when he fell into the creek"; this being in the year 1812, this boy was two years old when his mother was married; and he may have been six months old when he was taken from North Carolina, but it is not likely that he was older.

Then his stay in Kentucky up to the time his mother married Tom Lincoln was about a year and a half. This would give the actual year of Mr. Lincoln's birth in the neighborhood of 1804. And I would suggest it was really on the same day of the month as popularly given, but in another year. Then it would be in reality, February 12, 1804.

Now, we claim that the Kentucky chronology corroborates this change and the childhood life of Lincoln demands such a change, and, further, that the very physical life of this boy absolutely demands this change to give room for the real boy.

Without this change, chaos reigns over all the boyhood life of this great man. And it is nothing less than historical slaughter and vandalism to evade, side step and dodge the plain truth, on account of the moral, social, or political blemishes which might be brought to light in presenting the true record. If history fails to agree with itself, it is not history and should be discarded.

When it is shown that there are (historically) in the State of Kentucky eleven different birthplaces, four different log cabins, and at least twenty different "Nancy Hankses" each claiming priority, is it any wonder that a wrong "birthday" would also appear for this boy?

Thus it would appear that the real truth has been obscured, largely by those who should love and honor her most of all; but those have said, "away with her, she is not fit to live"; and they have taken her out and crucified her upon the Cross of false modesty.

And one late writer, fearing lest there might be a resurrection and a "hereafter," took his "spade" and dug the grave so deep that its bottom was cracked and smoked from the sulphurous fire of Gehena's flames. But Truth is a part of the framework of the Universe, and like the light of the sun cannot be buried (Barton, p. 322).

3. One more story illustrating the supernatural powers of the small boy, Abe Lincoln, is given by his schoolmate, Austin Gallaher. Austin says, "Abe often went to mill, carrying a half bushel of corn, and after it was ground he carried it back seven miles on his shoulder, making a fourteen-mile trip." And the majority of historians believe he did this.

Now, this was entirely too much for a little fellow under eight years old. And he could not have been older, if he were born in 1809. For he, with the family, left the State in 1816. The truth is that this boy was not less than eleven or twelve years old at this time, and at this age he could have carried the corn to mill, as related by his school-mate, for he was born February 12, 1804, on Puzzle Creek near Forest City, Rutherford County, in North Carolina.

In all these early stories, there is perfect correlation. They all fit perfectly into the North Carolina traditions, which of course were independent stories, and this could not have happened if those stories had been false.

CHAPTER SIXTEEN

"Filtering" Stories At Hodgensville

It was a very peculiar coincidence which the historians met with over at Hodgensville, Kentucky, where the great monument now stands, pointing out the place where Abraham Lincoln was not born.

Dr. Barton tells us what happened to him, even before he reached the noted town of Hodgensville, in search of book material. As he was going into the town on the train he discovered a gentleman who lived there, and had "lived there all his life" Dr Barton had taken his "spade" along and was eager to have a chance to "bury" every adverse story he ran across. Dr. Barton asked this gentleman what the good folks of the town of Hodgensville thought about Abraham Lincoln. Who was his father? And the reply was, immediately, that the father of Abraham Lincoln was "Abe Enloe"! All I know is what all the old folks used to say, and they all said that the father of Lincoln was Abe Enloe. I never heard them give any reason, or tell how they knew, but they all knew the story and believed it. "Some say he was born in Elizabethtown, and some say he was born somewhere else and moved here."

After a lengthy bombardment of this astonishing Kentucky

psychology by this historian, who wants to get this "buried" before he leaves it, he tells us that this kind of information did not originate in Hodgensville; "it filtered in from the outside world." He declares that it must have been in 1860 when the folks whom he speaks of as "Copperheads," started this scandal! Now it happens that the "Copperhead" is a bad snake. He doesn't manufacture any stories, nor does he evade the plain truth, but he will certainly fight you for what he believes to be his inalienable rights! Nor did he start any scandal or lies about Mr. Lincoln. And it is just as reprehensible to lie about the "Copperheads" as it is to lie about Mr. Lincoln or any one else. I am in a position to know that the "Copperheads" did not start this story.

Instead of going ahead and making an effort to correlate all these very old stories as a good historian should do under such circumstances, this minister-historian earnestly endeavors to discredit all this part of the Lincoln history in flagrant violation of the primary rules of historical research. His "Courses in Theology and History" seem not to have helped him very much in either.

We will agree with Brother Barton upon one specific point, and that is that "these stories filtered into Hodgensville." And we have the evidence that they not only filtered into Hodgensville, but that they had also "filtered" into the town of Elizabethtown "from the outside." Yes, they had "filtered" into the State of Kentucky before Tom and Nancy were married! What on earth could prevent such filtering, when it was the truth that Abraham Lincoln was present at his mother's wedding; and "able to run around on the floor when Tom and Nancy were married," as told by the preacher who performed the ceremony, and as sworn to by one of the most prominent jurists of the State of Kentucky.

It was not any secret then; every lawyer in the State of Kentucky believed this report, which they all said came from the preacher! And this was talked in Lincoln's time and written in the papers in his time, and he made no reply to these stories, for he himself believed they were true.

Abraham Lincoln Tells It

The simple truth is that Lincoln himself knew that he had "filtered" from North Carolina as the son of Abraham Enloe and Nancy Hanks. And he told this to one of his special friends upon the eve of the election, who was starting upon a visit to Rutherford County, North Carolina to see his relatives. This Mr. Davis related the incident to the late Dr. Edgerton, M. D., of the town of Hendersonville, with whom the two gentlemen, Davis and his friend, stayed all night on this trip back home. Lincoln said to Davis, "My mother is from Rutherford County, and my right name is Enloe, but I have always gone by the name of my stepfather" (Cathey, p. 86). While he knew it would hurt him in the North, he knew this news whispered around in Rutherford County, North Carolina, could do no harm down there (Cathey, p. 86).

But it did do him harm at some places in the north, where this was known during his campaign. This was talked in La Rue County extensively where the Lincolns had lived after Thomas and Nancy were married; it had been told all over the country that "Little Abe" was present at his own mother's wedding, and it could not be successfully denied there. For there were people then living who knew it to be true. Now, historians can dispute this, and the old people are all dead who were the witnesses in this case. That method has been sometimes employed in very important lawsuits. The defense lawyers manage to "continue, and to continue" the case until some of the most important witnesses are dead.

But this is anything else but the proper method of writing true history. These old people had some foundation for their conduct at the election, when they, the majority of them Republicans or Whigs, "refused to vote for Mr. Lincoln, because they claimed he was an illegitimate." This was not a good reason for their non-support, but it was the reason they assigned at the time. And they were then in position to know whether this were true or false. They were better informed then than any historian can be now, in regard to all such matters. Because the witnesses were living then, but they are dead now.

But the present historian must face the embarrassing situation of having this old "record" to meet in La Rue County, Kentucky.

And this same peculiar situation developed in North Carolina, during the Lincoln-Douglas campaign. Willis Bradley, a well-to-do planter in Rutherford County, who knew Lincoln's ancestors at that place, openly expressed himself as being in favor of Abraham Lincoln for President. And the people "taunted" Mr. Bradley, and tried to change his mind. But Bradley believed in the policies of Lincoln and said, "Lincoln was not responsible for what his parents or somebody did before he was born." "There was no way of disproving the charge made by the people at this time, that he was illegitimate" for they all knew it to be true (Mrs. Martha Keeter's story, this book).

Now, how did it happen that this North Carolina story gained currency here in this State, and at the same time a similar story was gaining like currency in La Rue County, Kentucky? Were both these independent stories manufactured by these same "Copperheads"? Or were there a bunch of these bad snakes denning at each separate location? But these serpents must have acted in collusion in this nasty business of spreading their slimy "slander" about Mr. Lincoln if this cloth came out of this kind of factory. Is it plausible, reasonable, and in keeping with good common sense to conclude that there was a secret conspiracy, covering this entire country, to defame the good name of this man of the hoe, the plow, the axe and the maul and wedge? Fools only are thus capable of such stultification. The foundation for these reports were laid in truth! There can be no other plausible answer to this question. It was not a political matter at all. And all the bombastic scribbling of prejudiced historians will no longer fool the people when the light is turned upon this question.

This ugly epithet, "Copperhead," was first used October 1, 1862, in the Cincinnati newspaper called the *Commercial*, after which it came rapidly into general acceptance as a term of opprobrium applied by Unionists during the Civil War to those who adhered rigidly to the Democratic organization and who were advocates of peace. It was especially popular in the Middle West, where it was applied to all Democrats, many of whom adopted it as a mark of honor, adopting as a badge the large copper cent of the time, bearing the head of "Liberty." The more radical opposed conscription, discouraged enlistment in the army, attacked the administration through the public press, and some were severely dealt with by the government. This term was also revived during the World War, and was applied to those who opposed the policies of the government (Nelson's *Encyclopaedia*).

CHAPTER SEVENTEEN

Dr. Barton's "Cuckoo's Nest"

It is a matter deeply to be regretted that such a brilliant and indefatigable historian as the late Dr. Barton should allow himself to become subservient to a political prejudice which would cause him to speak of reputable people as "Copperheads" and also to stoop to the point of casting reflections, innuendos and billingsgate at reputable people who have related incidents they either knew or believed to be true; and to speak slightingly and disparagingly of the North Carolina family of Enloes with whom Nancy Hanks, mother of Abraham Lincoln, made her home for a decade. Those who have noted the characteristics of a real historian will readily see that Dr. Barton has failed to measure up to the standard (Barton's *Paternity of Abraham Lincoln*, 231-243).

There was no occasion for such a willful perversion of the truth as found on page 231 of his encyclopedic and jumbled mass of his essay on Lincoln's origin. His little "Cuckoo's Nest" could just as easily be placed in the home of the Washingtons, Lees, Stonewall Jacksons, Bartons, Grants, Lincolns or any other family with equal disparagement to the other members of the same family; for there is no large family whose members all stand upon exactly the same intellectual level. So, it would have been nothing short of the miraculous for Abraham Enloe's children to all mount to such fame as this one born of a different mother! To what heights did the immediate kinfolks of Tom Lincoln ascend?

And Mr. Barton had before him Hon. James Cathey's book on Lincoln's origin, from which he made lengthy quotations in his book from page 74 to 98. And in this same book of Cathey's was an appraisal of the Enloes of America, showing the superior mentality of this stock of people, and that there had sprung from this old Scotch family of school teachers, educators, jurists, Congressmen, Senators, ministers, doctors and various leaders in different parts of the country. And Mr. Cathey challenges any who may be skeptically inclined to investigate for himself (Cathey's *Truth Is Stranger Than Fiction*, pp. 162-177).

This statement that these North Carolina Enloes "smirched" the name of their grandfather "to bolster up a fictitious relation to President Lincoln" is an inexcusable piece of misrepresentation. And no one so prejudiced is fit to have a place upon a jury in the "trial" of such a case, for the evidence fails to reveal any such an intent upon their part. But the fact is that just the opposite was the effort upon the part of the members of this family.

The Enloe Family is Ashamed of the Scandal

The members of Enloe's family were "ashamed" of this report, first circulated by their neighbors and other people of North Carolina, related as the granddaughter of Lincoln's aunt Martha Enloe was my own mother. I had graduated from college before I knew anything about this story. And after hearing this related by her uncle, a very old man, who claimed that he personally knew Lincoln's mother when she was in the home of his "uncle Abraham" Enloe, I expressed my grave doubts as to the reality of the facts. And the old man, with his eyes filled with tears after tragically telling of the "terrible fight" his uncle had with Tom Lincoln, and that it was reported that "poor Nancy" died of a broken heart and from the abuse of Tom Lincoln, he said to me, "Jim, if you don't believe what I say, go home and ask your mother and she will tell you just what I have"! And upon returning home I immediately asked my mother in regard to this matter. And she very apologetically remarked that it was "all true," but that the family was "ashamed" of it; that her uncle Abraham was "regarded as a great man in his community," and this was the reason she had never "whispered it" to any of her children. And to insinuate that this was told by these Enloes with any degree of gusto is absolutely false.

Old General Theodore Davidson, who settled the Enloe estate, relates the following: After this news had been circulated, a New York paper sent a reporter down to interview the Enloe family; and before they would agree to an interview, it was decided that they had better get together and talk over this matter that the gentleman from New York desired to talk about.

And after talking over the matter for some time, they told the New York reporter that they had nothing to say. And he went back to New York without any big headlines for his paper about this "Enloe family." This story of General Davidson will be given in full further on in this book.

In support of this statement, I have a letter written by Mr. J.G. Smith of Atlanta, a few years ago, who was at that time the head and proprietor of the "largest school book emporium in the South" and, after offering congratulations upon my book, *Abraham Lincoln, a North Carolinian*, Mr. Smith said, "Some years ago I lived next door to a family in which stayed a Miss Enloe, who stated that while their relation to President Lincoln was conceded, yet for a long time the family was afraid to proclaim it."

Knowing something of the very bitter sectional feeling at that time, I am very sure his North Carolina relatives would have been the last people in the world to "feel proud" of being akin to President Lincoln, some of whom only mentioned his name with very bitter profanity. And I have the statement of one of his half sisters, showing this kind of animus, "I know he is my half brother, but I hate Abraham Lincoln worse than I hate a rattlesnake"! Then, for a historian to so forget his mission as to misrepresent the very people of whom he should tell the absolute truth, is inexcusable.

Picture of Scroop Enloe,
Half-Brother of Lincoln

This is a picture of Scroop Enloe, son of Abraham Enloe. One can see great strength of character in this face, which is said to have been very much like that of his father, Abraham Enloe, and a man noted for intelligence, honesty, and charity to people who were in need of help. "No man ever came to him and was turned away."

CHAPTER EIGHTEEN

The Abbreviated Abraham Lincoln

We read of abbreviating the locks of long-haired Sampson, one of the Judges of ancient Israel which resulted in "putting out his eyes and giving him a job grinding in the prison mill." But they do more to Abraham Lincoln, this young "giant," than to deprive him of long hair. For his hair was not in the way; it was his size! He was just too big and too old to suit the history makers, and they proceeded to trim him down to fit the situation. They invented all kinds of machinery for this purpose, for they wanted to do a neat job. They wanted their machinery to be able to dress a youngster down to a size, and turn him out free from all marks and defects so that his own people would not be able to detect the slightest difference between him and the real person.

The first stroke of the regenerating machine cuts off five years of Lincoln's early life at one clip; and this amputated part of the boy is carefully and stealthily hidden in the thick underbrush of the social and political dismal swamp of the time. The next step is to abbreviate his age and physical capacity to correspond with his changed personality. This done, he is given a new "birthday," February 12, 1809!

Now, we can have some foundation for a conjecture as to

the time when this work began. It may not have begun till he entered into practice. There was a very strong temptation at the time it was done to detract the attention of the public from the persistent story that Mr. Lincoln was an "illegitimate." And if it had not been done prior to his entrance into politics it was done as a shield from such constant abuse and burning epithets as he knew would be constantly hurled at him in all his future campaigns. And Lincoln was mentally very alert; he knew this was true, and he might just as well prepare for this very kind of an attack. For this assault would certainly be used by his enemies, and their name was legion. But proof is lacking for this.

Again, it has been suggested, and not without considerable plausibility, that this change was made while the Lincoln family lived in Kentucky "to shield his mother from slanderous reports." And we are sure it was done for one of the two reasons here assigned, either of which would have been a sufficient cause. And we will offer the proof later that his mother did need just such a "protection" from the stinging tongues of the community. And while all kinds of "affidavits" are gotten up after Nancy is dead, to clear her name from reproach, as is usual in all such cases, it was a fact that the old "snuff box" crones did tattle about this poor mother of little "Abe." And it is all a waste of paper and time to build such a high wall of defense around the moral and social life of Tom Lincoln's wife after she came to Kentucky and married Tom Lincoln. No one has made any attack upon her for any immoral conduct as a wife. And all this great array of defense artillery is only wasted effort. Such work can only serve as target practice for immature marksmen.

While efforts have been made by historians to detour from Abraham Lincoln's request, made to the Chicago publisher, sidetracking the matter from Lincoln to his mother, this will not work. It was something about Lincoln that Scripps wanted, and not about Lincoln's mother.

Yet they will tell us that this "secret" which Mr. Lincoln confided to Mr. Scripps was that Lincoln's mother was an "illegitimate." But here Mr. Lincoln very probably "came clean" with Scripps and told him the plain truth, that he himself was an "illegitimate," and requested that Scripps would "not publish this fact at this time"! Lincoln knew there would be no use in his making the race for the Presidency or any other high office, if this fact were published to the world. He knew it would dig his political grave! And Abraham Lincoln was really very ambitious for power; for political honors of the highest character. It was in him as an essential element of his personality. This trait was inherited along with other strong family characteristics of high-blooded ancestors on both sides. (Ribot on *Heredity*)

A very peculiar name in Lincoln's ancestry on the Enloe side is that of "Scroop," an ensignia of honor away back in English history, when there were Lords of England by the name of "Scroop." And Abraham Lincoln's uncle Scroop (Enloe) became a noted Presbyterian minister. And I now have a large picture of Lincoln's half brother by the name of Scroop. And people claim this picture greatly resembles Abraham Lincoln.

Then, it would appear as a dernier resort, to save absolute and ignominious defea politically, the only thing Lincoln could do was to set up a fictitious birthday. It was a successful piece of strategy which worked splendidly, and Mr. Lincoln was elected President.

Lincoln a Hunter

The unabbreviated Lincoln was quite a hunter. As related in Miss Tarbell's *History of Lincoln* (Vol. I, pp. 14-16; see also Nicolay and Hay, Vol. I, p. 27), "Austin Gollaher and young Abe hunted coons and ran the woods together (Austin 11 and Abe 8 years old). Young Lincoln had his dog and ax, and when the dog would run a rabbit into a tree Abe would chop it out."

This is the real boy at the age when he fell into the creek. Here is the full text of this story by his playmate, Austin Gollaher:

> Abe and I had been going to school together for more than a year. Then school disbanded on account of there being so

few scholars, and we did not see each other for a long while.

One Sunday my mother visited the Lincoln's and I was taken along. Abe and I played around all day. Finally we concluded to cross the creek to hunt for some partridges young Lincoln had seen the day before. The creek was swollen by a recent rain, and, in crossing on the narrow foot-log Abe fell in. Neither of us could swim.

I got a long pole and held it out to Abe, who grabbed it. Then I pulled him ashore. He was almost dead, and I was badly scared. I rolled and pounded him in good earnest. Then I got him by the arms and shook him, the water meanwhile was pouring out of his mouth. By this means I succeeded in bringing him to, and he was soon all right.

Then a new difficulty confronted us. If our mothers discovered our wet clothes, they would whip us. This we dreaded from experience, and determined to avoid it.

It was June, the sun was very warm, and we soon dried our clothing by spreading it on the rocks about us. We promised never to tell the story, and I never did till after Lincoln's tragic death.

It will be remembered that Austin Gollaher made the statement to Mr. Brown, an interviewer, in 1886 that he, Gollaher, saved Lincoln's life from drowning in the year 1812 (Warren).

And Austin, Lincoln's playmate, says they had been going to school more than a year. This is the real boy. But when the "reducing machine" gets through with this boy who can hunt and chop rabbits out of trees, and go to school, and go to the mill with a half bushel of corn on his shoulder seven miles and back in a day, he is a very small boy unable to do any of these big-boy stunts. For he is "made up" to fit the fictitious date "1809." And, of course, this date must stand if it annihilates the boy.

This will probably throw some light upon the subject often mentioned by historians, in regard to Lincoln's embarrassment when the question of his boyhood in Kentucky was mentioned. Mr. Herndon, Lincoln's law partner, says: "It was with the greatest reluctance and embarrassment that Lincoln would speak of these experiences." Now, one who is not prejudiced can see the reason for such an unhappy situation. The natural boy was put into a "reducing machine" and it hurt him. It was like going to the guillotine to even mention his boyhood experiences to Abraham Lincoln, who really wanted to tell the real truth and live the real truth all the time.

Had he been a boy or a man of bad heart, this would never have troubled him; he never would have felt "embarrassed" over telling an untruth, and one as insignificant as the date for a boy's birthday. But this was a man, like his father, of a good heart by nature. And it choked him almost to death to give sanction to a fictitious origin. But this helped him to hold up his head among the big people of the world; to gain the power he craved, and above all to be in the extremely delicate position of welding back the broken links in the family of the American republic.

Now, there is only one of two theories we can adopt in regard to this whole matter, and that is: We must claim that Lincoln was a real boy and had part in these various performances as are related by the oldest and first historians of Mr. Lincoln, or we are forced to the absurd theory that Lincoln was not like other folks; that he was without any childhood, a "Melchizadek, without beginning of days."

Once more this great machine is used, and it is when this young man is grown, about twenty-one or two years old. They find that it works on a man as well as on a boy. And when he comes out he is only "17 years old"! If they could use this as successfully upon women as men this machine would sell for millions of dollars! But it would soon be used so much it would wear out.

Rothchild Herndon, in describing this machine making "Lincoln 17 years old," says, "as early as the eleventh year began the remarkable development in physique which culminated before he had reached his seventeenth birthday, at that time, having attained his full height, within a fraction of six feet and four inches. At which time he had the strength of a young giant" (*Master of Men*, p. 9).

As it is claimed that he was not an abnormal youth, it was

too early for his adolescent age to begin at eleven. This is unnatural for the ordinary, or average, boy.

And no normal youth or boy reaches his full manhood by seventeen. This is unnatural! And it did not occur. This is the machine-made boy, and starting at the popular date, 1809, it turns him out branded "17 years old"! Of course he was the "strange young man of a sad face"; and such performances were enough to make any good, honest boy feel "sad."

And this status may also throw some light upon the old story that, after the death of his mother, "Lincoln ran away from his home, and joined a flat-boat crew on the Mississippi River." Though it is claimed that Tom's brutal treatment of the boy caused him to leave home (Horton's *Youth's History of The Great Civil War*, 1st w.).

But, if his birthday had already been fixed as a "protection" to his mother, he would have sense enough to understand that he will be legally bound to Tom Lincoln till he is actually twenty-six! Thus giving this old "brute" five good years of his hard work!

Lincoln's Moving Speech Before a Jury

I am always moved to tears when I read about Abraham Lincoln's speech before the jury in a noted murder trial, in which he told of his once being "a poor, homeless boy, without friends, and the mother of the accused took him in and fed, clothed and gave him a home." He was in tears as he related this touching story, as was also the jury, and he won the case! The "brutality" and the extra five years to spend with the "brute" certainly would cause a boy to want to run away! (Herndon and Weik, Vol. II, p. 27).

This is given by Mr. Lincoln's partner as "one of the most gratifying triumphs of Lincoln's life. And we shall give the reader the full text of this touching story.

> The trial of William Armstrong for the murder of James P. Metzger in May, 1858, at Beardstown, Illinois, in which Lincoln secured the acquittal of the defendant, was gratifying to Lin-

THE EUGENICS OF PRESIDENT ABRAHAM LINCOLN 149

coln. Lincoln's defense, wherein he floored the principal prosecuting witness who had testified positively to seeing the fatal blow struck in the moonlight by showing from an almanac that the moon had set, was not more convincing than his eloquent and irresistible appeal in his client's favor. The latter's mother, old Hannah Armstrong, the friend of his (Lincoln's) youth, had solicited him to defend her son.

He told the jury [relates the prosecuting attorney] of his once being a poor, friendless boy; that Armstrong's parents took him into their own house, fed and clothed him, and gave him a home. There were tears in his eyes as he spoke. The sight of his tall, quivering frame, and the particulars of the story he so pathetically told, moved the jury to tears also, and they forgot the guilt of the defendant in their admiration of his advocate. It was the most touching scene I ever witnessed.

This story was furnished to the historian Herndon, by Mr. J. Henry Shaw, the prosecuting attorney on the other side of the case. After this trial was over, Mrs. Armstrong was informed of the verdict; and she said:

Lincoln had said to me, "Hannah, your son will be cleared before sundown." I left the court-room, and they came and told me my son was cleared and a free man. I went up to the court house. The jury shook hands with me, and so did the judge and Lincoln; tears streamed down Lincoln's eyes.... After the trial, I asked him what his fee would be; told him I was poor. "Why, Hannah," he said, "I sha'n't charge you a cent, and anything else I can do for you, I will do it willingly and without charge." He afterward wrote to me about a piece of land certain men were trying to get from me and said, "Hannah, they can't get your land. Let them try it in the circuit court and then you appeal it; bring it to the supreme court and I and Herndon will attend to it for nothing."

Now, we ask the reader. Why did Lincoln tell this kind of a story? A story which in substance cast reflections upon "his own dear father," if Tom Lincoln were his father! Why was it that he war, a "poor, homeless boy." From what the late historians have to say in praise of Thomas Lincoln, such was untrue. Lincoln was never without a good home with his own father; and Mr. Lincoln, the good-hearted lawyer in the above case was very simply lying to this jury! Can we think this?

Now, one of two things is absolutely true: Abraham Lincoln was guilty of a frame-up and was lying to this jury, or he was revealing a great big sore place in his life; he was telling the actual truth. He had found the situation at Tom Lincoln's after the death of his own mother so terrible, so unbearable, so "brutal," that it was impossible for him to remain at home any longer. He left home!

Tom put this boy out, "hired him out for a few cents a day," and kept all the money after they moved to Indiana, "Abraham being about eight years old." Yet this "good-sized boy was strong and could almost do the work of a man" (Ludwig). For he was five years to a day older than he is made to appear, counting from 1809.

He is nearing the age now when he will feel more keenly the galling yoke of old Tom's brutality; and his servitude for the man who had beaten his dear mother can be borne no longer! Poor child!

And it was the vivid recollection of these bitter, unforgettable days in this good man's life that made this strong man cry before the Armstrong jury. Yes, savage, barbarous conditions drove him off from where Tom lived; it was not a home, rather it was the cage of a Bengal tiger, or the stall for a Kentucky ass! Abraham Lincoln was homeless!

CHAPTER NINETEEN

Lincoln Apotheosized By Historians

In attacking our position, that Abraham Lincoln was born prior to all his Kentucky experiences we have been reminded of the fact that Abraham Lincoln himself said he was born "February 12, 1809."

Now, in the minds of some people, if it can be shown that Lincoln did make this statement, it forever settles the question. For it was impossible for "Honest Abe" to tell anything under any kind of circumstances but the absolute truth. Other people, great and small, can and do, under extreme pressure of circumstances, side-step the facts a little when there is a very great deal involved. But the "Cherry Tree Stories" of George Washington and Abraham Lincoln are proof to the historians that here are two men who never deviated in the very smallest fraction from the absolute truth. This makes good reading for the young people! These men are such fine examples for the boys, it is claimed. And they certainly are.

But did it ever occur that there is a place and a time for putting out the Cherry Trees? And that these should never become the basic facts upon which history is built. History should be founded upon well ascertained data which correlates with all essential and related facts. There should appear no incongruities in the general course of historical development. In other words, history should be in harmony with itself! There should be a perfect correlation between all physical, mental, moral, sociological and chronological elements which form the essential fabric.

And in any apparent conflict between apocryphal chronology and the natural, physical and mental elements entering in as primary factors, rather than destroy the history, change the chronology! For the controlling factor is not chronology, but life! The doubtful chronology cannot force one to a change of his life but a change in the life will force a change in the questioned chronology. For the life predominates over any and all chronological data, especially when they appear in conflict.

Now I submit this as a fundamental principle of historical research, and ask that this be applied to the subject under consideration.

1. We are not able to change the actual, physical and mental life of Abraham Lincoln as he lived this life here in the world. And when, by the common consent of friends, playmates and early associates, who as disinterested parties at the time of relating the various and sundry experiences with themselves and others, a guileless and innocent chain or series of facts related by Lincoln and many others, such statements should be accepted in preference to any apocryphal date that would conflict with the basic factors.

2. If this rule were followed, the fictitious date, 1809, would be set aside. For we can much more easily dispose of this date than we can give up his life. And more especially does this become apparent when there is a date mentioned in connection with the life happenings, 1812, which corroborates every event of the life; and all the circumstances, including the date itself (Gollaher).

3. Then, when a date appears in connection with the life stories, all in accord with each other, and this appears to be in conflict with another date, the one in harmony with the life history should prevail, and the other should be set aside as a fictitious date. The story of Lincoln, of his catching a fish and giving it to a

soldier in 1812, supports the Gollaher story of 1812.

Now, if the historians will not subscribe to this principle of criticism, the intelligent readers will! For this is the only thing for the honest investigators to do if they are really seeking all the truth.

The Popular Date of Lincoln's Birth is Untenable

The fact that some late writers, exceedingly anxious to submerge all the Lincoln boyhood stories in conflict with the popular date of Lincoln's birth, have dug up the very old "grannie" with a big congregation of others, who "claim they were there" at Hodgensville on the very night of Abraham Lincoln's birth, fails to lend much weight.

1. In thus producing this "array of evidence" in support of this as the real place and time of Lincoln's birth, it would appear that all these witnesses have been "seen" in regard to this question and have discussed with the historians the matter of Lincoln's "illegitimacy," before the evidence was taken down, which would furnish the foundation for bias in this testimony.

2. And it is contended that Lincoln said he was born here in 1809.

But if he made another statement in the quiet of a social, friendly conversation with an old friend which is contradictory or at irreconcilable conflict with a statement made under the heavy pressure of the political campaign with the view to publication, the former should be accepted as true, and the latter rejected as fictitious. For the statement made for "political propaganda" could not be free from bias under the known circumstances. And the same may be said of the old neighbors who make affidavit to being present at Lincoln's birth.

Especially should we accept as true the statement of Abraham Lincoln when this statement is in perfect harmony with another chronology, given free from any political influence, and is itself endorsed by other unbiased witnesses, who at that time, like Lincoln, were not thinking of these statements being published.

3. All these conditions appear in the statements:

A) Of Lincoln himself to Judge Helm, that he remembered going to the store in Elizabethtown and eating brown sugar (before 1809).

B) Of Judge Helm, that he remembered feeding Lincoln brown sugar at the old store in Elizabethtown (before 1809).

C) Of Haycraft, the historian, who said, he remembered Abraham Lincoln at Elizabethtown when he was very small, walking around with his mother in his shirttail (before 1809).

D) Of Austin Gollaher, with whom Lincoln went to school, who said, he saved Abraham Lincoln from drowning in 1812, and at that time he and Lincoln had been in school more than a year. And that they as boys hunted together.

E) Of Rev. John Duncan, who helped Lincoln catch a ground hog.

F) Of Austin Gollaher, who told of Lincoln carrying the corn to mill.

Now, if this 1809 is a correct date, then all these other statements are absolutely false, and so is the date given by Austin Gollaher, Lincoln's chum and playmate. These things could not happen if Lincoln had been born in 1809, as that would be two years before he was born when he ate the sugar.

But the great weight of evidence is on the side of all these playmates and also Lincoln, who acknowledged eating the sugar! So, he must have been born at the time, which corresponds to these stories. There is no escape from this logic! And he must have been about 8 years old in 1812, when Austin Gollaher pulled him out of Knob Creek, saving him from drowning.

Then, in the event that this suggested change is made, discarding the date in history, "February 12, 1809," what will be the result? Well, in the first place, the record will be true. And that is what the people demand, as Lincoln is not in politics now. His great stirring campaigns are over, and there is no use in keeping right on making false statements just to help him to be elected. His election is all over, and he has made the country a great President; a situation which would have been impossible had it not been for this false date, giving him legitimacy. It was then a necessary expedient in his political career as it would have been impossible for this man, great and good as he was at heart, to carry his heavy cross up the White House steps and unload it in the nation's Capitol!

Also, let this fact be observed in our consideration of this difficult Lincoln situation, that however high Mr. Lincoln may have climbed upon his own ladder before the eyes of the American people yet with all his good qualities he was neither angel nor God. He was simply a mortal man, made up of our common clay. And as I think of him now, my own flesh and blood, I am quite sure it could not please him to be a subject of glorification by historians or anybody else. He should not become apotheosized and deified as one immune to mistakes. We make ours; and Lincoln made his, for we all are mortal here below.

The Grave Of Nancy Hanks, Lincoln's Mother

Here quietly rests the sacred dust of the "orphan" Nancy Hanks, the child of "mystery," who, driven away from the Enloe home to become the most grief-stricken of all the world's "Hagars," and whose gift upon the country's golden altar was more precious than any ever offered, save the world's propitiatory sacrifice upon Mount Calvary!

CHAPTER TWENTY

The Death Of Lincoln's Mother

It is claimed that the mother of Abraham Lincoln died in the year 1818, October 5. Hers was a short life, though a life quite replete with sorrow mingled with tears and severe hardships.

And her sad face, like that of her noble son, constantly bore the indelible stamp of her inner feelings. Her poor life was ground out in a tread mill; yea, in the prison-mill of the "subnormal-minded" Thomas Lincoln the supposed ancestor of a real man! Let all who will scowl and frown at this indictment; the evidence which I have will sustain it. His own son-in-law, Col. Chapman, testifies that "Thomas Lincoln treated little Abe with great brutality," and B.H. Melton, my mother's uncle, whose own mother was Lincoln's aunt Martha Enloe, stated to me that "old Tom" was brutal to Nancy's boy and her too; that upon one occasion he "beat her till the blood ran down to her shoes"! He had secured this information from the original sources, and it was true. This old man knew Lincoln's mother while she was in the home of the Enloes in North Carolina.

But the condoning historians have been busy for some time grooming this illiterate bear into a very decent-looking gentleman. They tell us "he sat upon juries," took one or two contracts as a carpenter, though he failed to get the logs of the building the same length, and he was appointed "road overseer" at one time. But some of us know there are some very "poor sticks" who can get on a jury at times, as this is sometimes the very kind of material wanted. And it did not require much intellect or a man of good character in his home to help chop trees and dig dirt in constructing a primitive Kentucky road. There is more in that one short statement from Col. Chapman than in everything all the historians have been able to get together in revealing Tom Lincoln's true character. "He was very brutal!" If they continue, they may yet have Tom very well educated and a Lieutenant Governor of Kentucky.

Their explanation of the charge of "brutality" by furnishing the example or case in point, where Thomas slapped little Abe off the fence for speaking to a man passing the road is not a start; it may be but a small intimation of the things not written, but strongly intimated. Therefore, their conclusion from the premises in this case, furnishes an example of the *"fallacia consequentis"* as to Tom's "brutality."

The above brief discussion has paved the way for some things now to follow in regard to the death of Lincoln's mother. There has been some cloud or mystery overshadowing this matter ever since the death of this woman. There was something that caused Tom's neighbors to "talk a lot," it was related by the old people. And while it occasionally happens that unguarded remarks are made by neighbors under such circumstances, in this case there really appears to be some foundation for a current and very stubborn report reflecting upon Thomas Lincoln, the husband.

It had seeped out that Tom Lincoln was not happy with his wife, Nancy; and that he often had "pouty" spells (Wayne Wipple). And it was told by a close relative of the Enloes that it was "Tom's jealousy" that lay at the very foundation of his "brutality" to Nancy and her little boy (B.H.M.)

The very esprit de corps of this Lincoln home seems to grow more gloomy as the long days pass. Mr. Herndon, the historian, has made the astonishing statement that Abraham Lincoln "had an inside cancer," metaphorically speaking, and we may not misjudge if we infer that his "cancer" came in part at least from his mother. In fact the son's "cancer" came from his mother, who had a bad "cancer" growing and daily eating away in her heart! And it has been claimed that there is no cure for a cancer but death!

So, in the autumn, some say, when the flowers and leaves turn golden on the Kentucky hills, the strange malady called "milk sickness" got its start, and caused a number of deaths in the community where the Lincoln family lived. And Nancy, Tom's wife, was already sick with a large, incurable cancer, and in a short while she grew to be worse and fever soon followed, and Tom told the neighbors that his wife had "milk sickness"; her death followed in just a short while. And I doubt not that Tom himself did some of the "talking about cancer."

Her passing was not unexpected to this mother of this fine boy. She called him to her bedside for a farewell talk, giving him her parting words, "I am going away, Abraham; read your Bible and be a good boy; be kind to everybody, and meet me in Heaven"! And the soul of Nancy Hanks Lincoln flew out from under the earthly shadows.

But after the death of this unfortunate mother, the old people would get together and talk in little groups. People must have something to talk about. And in these private conversations, these neighbors did not exonerate Thomas Lincoln from all blame in his wife's death. It was thought by some that there was a "worse" sickness than the "milk sickness" that contributed to the death of Tom's wife. And this was "grief"! This woman died from grief and the rough treatment she received from Tom Lincoln (B. H. Melton). And I shall never forget the deep feeling of the old man who, in tears, related this to me in regard to the cause of Nancy's death. He knew all the "inside" stories.

This Melton story is not without its historical background and foundation in an old Kentucky affidavit, for a long time suppressed. We dig this reference to community gossip from the old affidavit of Dr. C.C. Graham centogenarian, who made affidavit that he was at the wedding of Thomas Lincoln and Nancy Hanks.

Dr. Graham's Affidavit In Full

The following affidavit by Dr. Christopher Columbus Graham was procured by Mr. Henry Whitney Cleveland, and written by Mr. Cleveland and signed by Dr. Graham. It was published in the Louisville *Courier-Journal* and other papers and with a very significant omission, in some histories (Barton, pp. 337-343).

I, Christopher Columbus Graham, now in my hundredth year, and visiting the Southern Exposition in Louisville where I live, tell this to please my young friend, Henry Cleveland, who is nearly half my age. He was often at the Springs Hotel in Harrodsburg, Kentucky, then owned and kept by me for invalids and pleasure seekers. I am one of the two living men who can prove that Abraham Lincoln, or Linkhorn, as the family was miscalled, was born in lawful wedlock, for I saw Thomas Lincoln marry Nancy Hanks on the twelfth day of June, 1806. He was born at what was then known at the Rock Spring Farm, it is now called the Creal Place, three miles south of Hodgensville, in La Rue County, Kentucky.

Kentucky was first a county of Virginia, after its settlement, and was then divided into three counties; and these again divided are pretty much the present State. The first historian was Filson, who made and published the first map of the separate territory, with the names of streams and stations as given by Daniel Boone and Squire Boone, James Harrod and others. I knew all these as well as President Lincoln's parents.

I think they lived on the farm four years after he was born. Another boy was born at Hodgensville, or, I should say, buried there. The sister, Sally, was older than Abe, I think. I think the paper now owned by Henry Cleveland is the "marriage lines" written by Rev. Jesse Head, a well-known Methodist preacher. I do not think the old Bible it was found in was that of Tom Lincoln. It would cost too much for him. All of the records in it were those of the father's family, the John M. Hewetts, of the wife of Dr. Theodore S. Bell. Dr. Bell was only about twenty years younger than I am, and probably got the certificate in 1858 or 1860 when assertions were made that Tom Lincoln and Nancy Hanks

THE EUGENICS OF PRESIDENT ABRAHAM LINCOLN   161

were not married when Abe was born.

He was reputed to have been born February 12, 1809, and I see no good reason to dispute it. Sally, I am sure, was the first child, and Nancy was a fresh and good-looking girl, I should say past twenty. Nancy lived with the Sparrow family a good bit. It was likely Tom had the family Bible from Virginia, through his father, called Abraham Linkhorn. His brothers, however, were older, if they were brothers and not uncles, as some say. I was hunting roots for my medicines and just went to the wedding to get a good supper, and got it.

Bibles cost as much as the spinning wheel, the loom, or rifle, and were imported in the main. A favorite with the Methodists was Fletcher's, or one he wrote a preface for. Preachers used it and had no commentaries. A book dedicated to King James, or any other king did not take well in the Revolutionary times. The Bibles I used to see had no printed records or blanks, but a lot of fine linen handmade paper would be bound in front and back. On this, family history and land matters were written out fully like a book. Some had fifty pages. The court houses even were made out of logs, and the meeting houses too, if they had any. No registers were kept as in English parish churches, and are not yet. Before a license could be had, a bond and security was taken of the bridegroom and the preacher had to return to the Court all marriages of the year. This was often a long list, and at times papers were lost or forgotten, but not often. The "marriage lines" given by the preacher to the parties were very important in case the records were burned up by accident. Such is the paper that Henry Cleveland has shown me. The ring was not often used, as so few had one. The Methodist church discipline forbid "the putting on of gold or costly apparel," and I think a preacher with a gold watch, if not an inherited one, would have been dismissed. A preacher that married was "located," and that ended his itinerancy in the Methodist church. The Presbyterians were educated and married; Baptists not educated.

Tom Lincoln was a carpenter, and a good one for those days when a cabin was built mainly with the ax, and not a nail or bolt or hinge in it, only leathers and pins to the door, and no glass except in watches and spectacles and bottles. Tom had the best set of tools in what was then and now Washington County. La Rue

County, where the farm was settled, was then Hardin.

Jesse Head, the good Methodist preacher who married them, was also a carpenter or cabinet maker by trade, and as he was then a neighbor they were good friends. He had a quarrel with the Bishops and was not an itinerant for many years, but an editor and county judge afterwards in Harrodsburg. Mr. Henry Cleveland has his commission from Governor Isaac Shelby.

Many of the great men of the south and the north were then opposed to slavery, mainly because the new Negroes were as wild as the Indians and might prove as dangerous. Few of the Whites could read, and yet Pope and Dryden and Shakespeare were as well known as Bunyan's *Pilgrim's Progress* and Baxter's *Saint's Rest*. Some were educated in Virginia and North Carolina before they came, and these, when they became teachers, wrote out their school books entirely by hand.

Thomas Lincoln, like his son after him, had a notion that fortunes could be made by trips to New Orleans by flatboat. This was dangerous, from snags and whirlpools in the rivers, from Indians, and even worse – pirates of the French, Canadians and half-breeds. Steam was unknown, and the flats had to be sold in New Orleans as they could not be rowed back against the current. The neighbors joked Tom for building his boat too high and narrow from an idea he had about speed that has since been adopted by ocean steamships.

But he lacked in ballast. He loaded her up with bear hams and buffalo, which last was then not so plenty for meat or hides as when the Boone brothers came in. Besides he had wax for bees which seemed to follow the White people, and he had mink and coon and beaver and wolf skins, gentian root (that folks then called "gensang" or sang), nuts, honey, peach brandy and whisky, and jeans woven by his wife and Sally Bush, whom he married after Nancy died.

Some said she died of heart trouble, from slanders about her and old Abe Enloe, called Inlow, while her Abe, named for the pioneer Abraham Linkhorn, was still little.

But I am ahead of my story, for Nancy had just got married where I was telling it, and the flatboat and Sally Bush Lincoln come in before he goes over to what people called "Indiany." I will finish that and then go back.

He started down Knob Creek when it was flush with rains; but the leaves held water like a sponge and the ground was shaded with big trees and papaw and sasafras thickets and "cain," as Bible-read folks spelt the cane, and streams didn't dry up in summer as they do now. When he got to the Ohio it was flush, too, and full of whirlpools and snags. He had his tool chest along, intending to stop and work in Indiana and take down another boat. But he never got to the Mississippi with that, for it upset, and he only saved his chest and part of the load because he was near to the Indiana shore. He stored what he saved under bark and came home afoot, and in debt to neighbors who had helped him. But people never pressed a man who lost by Indians or water.

Now I go back for a spell. Thomas and Nancy both could read and write, and little Abe went to school about a year. He was eight years old at the time of the accident to Tom Lincoln's down-the-river venture. Thomas and Nancy were good common people, not above nor below their neighbors, and I did not take much notice of them, because there was no likelihood that their wedding would mean more than other people's did.

The preacher, Jesse Head, often talked to me on religion and politics, for I always liked the Methodists. I have often thought it might have been as much from his free-spoken opinions as from Henry Clay's American-African colonization idea in 1817, that I lost a likely Negro man who was leader of my musicians. It is said that Tom Gorwin met him in Ohio on his way to Canada, and asked if I was along. The boy said, no, he was going for his freedom. Governor Corwin said he was a fool; he had never been whipped or abused, but dressed like a White man, with the best to eat, and that hundreds of White people would be glad of such a good place, with no care but cared for.

The boy drew himself up and said, "Mars Tom that situation with all its advantages is open to you if you want to go and fill it."

But Judge Head never encouraged any runaway nor had any "underground railroad." He only talked freely and boldly, and had plenty of true Southern men with him, such as Clay. The Eli Whitney cotton gin had now made slavery so valuable that preachers looked in Hebrew and Greek testaments for scripture for it.

Tom Lincoln and Nancy and Sally Bush were just steeped full of Jesse Head's notions about the wrong of slavery and the rights of man as explained by Thomas Jefferson and Thomas Paine. Abe Lincoln the Liberator was made in his mother's womb and father's brain and in the prayers of Sally Bush; by the talks and sermons of Jesse Head, the Methodist circuit rider, assistant County judge, printer-editor and cabinet maker, Little Abe grew up to serve as a cabinet maker himself two Presidential terms.

It was in my trip to Canada after my Negro that I met the younger brother of the great chief Tecumseh. A mob wanted to kill me because I was after my property that had legs and a level head. The Indian was one of the finest-looking men I ever saw, and in the full uniform of a British officer. He protected me and we had a talk after the trouble was over. He said that history was right about the death of his great brother Tecumseh at the battle of the Thames in 1813. But the story of his skin being taken off to make razor straps was all a lie, as they never had the chance. He was not even slain at the point in the battle indicated by Col. Richard M. Johnson, whose accession to the Vice-Presidency in 1836 was largely due to the credit which he gained for this supposed exploit. My Indian protector said he was a lad at the time, but was there; and that the red men never abandoned their chiefs, dead nor alive.

I come back again to the Lincoln-Hanks wedding of 1806. Rev. or Judge Jesse Head was one of the most prominent men there, as he was able to own slaves but did not on principle. Next, I suppose came Mordecai Lincoln, at one time a member of the Kentucky Legislature. He was a good Indian fighter, and although some say he was the elder brother of Tom Lincoln, I understand he was his uncle or father's brother. The story of his killing the Indian who killed old Abraham Lincoln is all "my eye and Betty Martin."

My acceptance of this whole pedigree is on hearsay, and none of it from the locality of Tom Lincoln's home. There is a Virginia Land Warrant No. 3,334, of March 4, 1780, for four hundred acres of land, cost one hundred and sixty pounds, located in Jefferson County, Kentucky, on Long Run, and signed by William Shannon, D.S.J.C. and William May, S. J.C. witnessed by Anniah Lincoln and Josiah Lincoln, C.C. (chain carrier), and Abraham Linkhorn, marker, dated May 7, 1785, five years later. "Mordecai Lincoln, Gentleman," is the title given one who died in Berks County, Pennsylvania in 1735, and his will is recorded in the Register's office in Philadelphia. New Jersey, Virginia and Tennessee also have the name correctly in the last century.

The fame of General Benjamin Lincoln of the Revolution was on every tongue at that time. In the field book of Daniel Boone, owned by Lyman C. Draper, five hundred acres of land was entered for Abraham Lincoln upon Treasury Warrant No. 5,994, December 11, 1782. The officers of the land office of Virginia could spell and so could the surveyor and deputy surveyor (Record "B," p. 60 of Jefferson County in 1785). The two chain-carriers spelled the name correctly. Why not also think the third man spelled his correctly? A very illiterate man could pronounce what he could not spell, and Abraham Linkhorn, who had money and could write, knew his own name.

President Lincoln told James Speed, "I don't know who my grandfather was, and am more concerned to know what his grandson will be." I am not sure that we know, either, perfectly well yet.

While you pin me down to facts, I will say that I saw Nancy Hanks Lincoln at her wedding, a fresh-looking girl, I should say over twenty. Tom was a respectable mechanic, and could choose, and she was treated with respect.... [something may be omitted here]

I was at the infare, too, given by John H. Parrott, her guardian – and only girls who had money had guardians appointed by the Court. We had bear meat (that you can eat the grease of, and it not rise like other fats); venison, wild turkey and ducks; eggs, wild and tame (so common you could buy them at two bits a bushel); maple sugar, swung on a string, to bite off for coffee or whiskey; syrup in big gourds; peach and honey; a sheep the two families barbecued whole over coals of wood burned in a pit and covered with green boughs to keep the juices in; and a race for the whiskey barrel. The sheep cost the most, and corn was early raised in what is now Boyle County, at the Isaac Shelby place. I don't know who stamped in the first peach seed, but they grew before the apples.

Our table was of the puncheons cut from the solid logs,

and the next day they were the floor of the new cabin.

It is all stuff about Tom Lincoln keeping his wife in an open shed in a winter when the wild animals left the woods and stood in the corners next the stick-and-clay chimneys, so as not to freeze to death; or, if climbers got on the roof. The Lincoln's had a cow and calf, milk and butter, a good feather bed for I have slept in it (while they took the buffalo robes on the floor because I was a doctor). They had home-woven "kiverlids," big and little pots, a loom and wheel; and William Hardesty who was there too, can say with me that Tom Lincoln was a man and took care of his wife.

I have been in back camps with Daniel and Squire Boone and James Harrod. We have had to wade in the "crick," as Daniel spelt it, to get our scent lost in the water, and the Indian dogs off our trail. When trailed and there was no water handy I have seen Daniel cut a big grapevine loose at the bottom with his tomahawk from the ground. Then, with a run and swing from the tree it hung to, swing and jump forty feet clear to break the scent on the ground. I have done it too, but not so far. He could beat any man on the run and jump, but it took more than two Indians or one bear to make him do it. If no dog barked in the silent woods, we could run backward very fast and make Mr. Indian think we had gone the way we came. They went that way and we the other for deer, scalps and hair. Squirrel barking or chattering at the Indians, or dogs, often told us of our danger. I wanted to have a pioneer exhibit at the great Louisville Southern Exposition of 1883 and 1884. I wanted the dense laurel and the papaw thickets planted in rich soil; the bear climbing the bee tree and beaten by the swinging log hung by the hunter in his way, the creeping Indian with his tomahawk and the hunter with the old flint-and-steel rifle, just as I had seen them. Then I wanted to have women from the mountains and the counties that railroads and turnpikes have not opened and have then in reality to spin and weave, or bead and fringe the moccasin, and hunting shirt and leggings as they did when I was a boy. This, by the side of the industries and arts of the new era, and the wool and cotton machinery in its present perfection, would indeed tell to the eyes of the changes seen by an old man who has lived a hundred years. As they did not listen to me I have asked Henry Cleveland, who was a boy and played with my children at Harrodsburg Springs in the forties, to write it as I talked it to him. I am very deaf, but can see and talk, and will now write my autograph to what he has written and copied off, and will take up James Harrod at another time.

>Christopher Columbus Graham
>in my hundredth year

I make this affidavit to vindicate the character of Thomas Lincoln and Nancy Hanks, and to put to rest forever the legitimacy of Abraham Lincoln's birth. I was formerly proprietor of the Harrodsburg Springs; I am a retired physician, and am now a resident of Louisville, Kentucky. I think Felix Grundy was also present at the marriage of said Thomas Lincoln and Nancy Hanks, the father and mother of Abraham Lincoln. The said Jesse Head, the officiating minister at the marriage afore said, afterward removed to Harrodsburg, Kentucky, and edited a paper there and died at that place.

>Christopher Columbus Graham

Subscribed and sworn to before me, this March 20, A.D. 1882

>N.C. Butler, Clerk United States
>Circuit Court, First District, Ind.
>By J.W. Wartman, Deputy Clerk

Dr. Graham's Affidavit

The following affidavit by Dr. Graham was procured by Captain J.W. Wartman, Deputy Clerk of the United States Circuit Court at Evansville, Indiana, in whose home Dr. Graham was visiting at the time:

I, Christopher C. Graham, now of Louisville, Kentucky, aged ninety-eight years, on my oath say: That I was present at the marriage of Thomas Lincoln and Nancy Hanks, in Washington County, near the town of Springfield, Kentucky; that one Jesse Head, a Methodist preacher of Springfield, Kentucky, performed the ceremony. I knew the said Thomas Lincoln and Nancy Hanks well, and know the said Nancy Hanks to have been virtuous and respectable, and of good parentage. I do not remember the exact date of the marriage, but was present at the marriage aforesaid; and I make this affidavit freely, and at the request of J.W. Wartman, to whom for the first time, I have this day incidentally stated the fact of my presence at the said wedding of President Lincoln's father and mother.

Scrutinizing the Affidavit

The foregoing lengthy and detailed statement of this aged doctor, together with his affidavit are regarded by historians as very important material bearing upon the question of Lincoln's legitimacy. And one does not have to be a "skilled fingerprintist" to be able to see in the affidavit, in the "saids" and "aforesaids" the special imprints of another hand guiding Dr. Graham at this time; the hand of the Deputy Clerk of the Circuit Court, J.W. Wartman.

We call the attention of the reader to the following specifications of this affidavit:

1. This was by a special request.

2. To vindicate the character of Thomas Lincoln and Nancy Hanks.

3. To put to rest forever the legitimacy of Abraham Lincoln's birth.

The necessity for an affidavit is occasioned by the persistent rumors all over the country that Abraham Lincoln was not the legal son of Thomas Lincoln; this having been started at the wedding, and has been published to the world many times, and "all the lawyers of any note in the State of Kentucky believe it."

Now this affidavit is made seventy-six years after Tom Lincoln and Nancy Hanks were married. And for the specific purpose of "putting to rest forever" the legitimacy of Abraham Lincoln's birth, which up to this time had not been "put to rest," and they secure this old herb and root "Doctor" with the hope that he will have the very medicine for this bad case. They have tried all the other "Doctors" they could find and their patient failed to get better. Of course, if anybody can make any new landing, it is hoped that "Christopher Columbus" will be able to do it. But the truth is that any one will have a very difficult job to tackle a case of 76 years standing!

And it was two years later when he made the other long statement quoted above; it was 78 years distant from the facts.

Now, let us notice a few statements in this centogenarian's lecture written out as he talked it off for the special benefit of Henry Whitney Cleveland, who writes it as Dr. Christopher Columbus Graham unrolls it from his fertile memory.

1. This also is to prove that Lincoln was a legitimate son of Thomas Lincoln, by showing that Tom and Nancy were married before Abraham Lincoln was born. As "there were assertions that Tom and Nancy were not married when Abraham was born," says this doctor.

The object and purpose of this lengthy writing was to put an end to these "assertions." The affidavit made two years before this didn't do much good. And now a long statement is made and it is published in the Louisville *Courier-Journal*, and later in Miss Tarbell's *History of Lincoln*.

It appears that many were thinking that Tom and Nancy had lived together for some time before they became "man and wife"; and to disprove this fact gave the historians a lot of work, and especially until after they found the record of the marriage which settled the question of a legal wedding.

The late historians were exceedingly anxious to get this fence built to fence in little Abraham with Tom Lincoln's family; and after working very hard and putting up a big, strong fence they will still find lots of trouble in keeping Nancy's boy inside this fence. For he was born on the outside of the fence and the discovery of records can not avail anything.

Now it would have been possible that this doctor was present and upon this occasion, of so many people, and the good things to eat and drink, including Tom's whisky and peach brandy it could happen that little "Abe" was not seen by this doctor. Neither the bride nor groom would pick up this boy and present him to the crowd, as a part of the future family of the Lincolns!

But the preacher saw him at this wedding and had been there before, doubtless, and he knew that this bright girl had a boy she called "Abe" before the marriage. And he told this to his special friends. Of course he had no idea that this youngster would some day become the President of the United States! But when the great Lincoln-Douglas campaign got into full blast, it revived all of these old slumbering stories. And preachers were employed and lawyers and judges, with divers "witnesses" to furnish affidavits galore in an effort to legitimatize Nancy's boy. They wanted "Cherry Tree Stories" that will have a good moral (?) effect upon the country.

The earliest historians, Mr. Herndon and Mr. Lamon, both began with the intention of giving the people the actual facts about Abraham Lincoln's origin, but these gentlemen, both great personal friends of Lincoln, as proven by their positions and relationships with Lincoln, met such an intolerable storm of abuse and invective that they desisted from their original purpose. Yet the many striking implications of these able writers lead to no other conclusion in the histories they have written; and they held in their possession much evidence that has not come to us, evidence which has been "suppressed and destroyed," upon which they based their first historical conclusions. Daniel in the lion's den was not in much greater jeopardy than these first historians who were hurled into the fiery furnace of persecution which was ten-fold hotter for them than for any others (Barton, pp. 367- 371).

However, it turns out that when they got this old Doctor to talking, he talked too much for the historians; he didn't know just when to stop nor what to omit, and told some things which were very undesirable. You note what he said about Lincoln's reference to "his grandfather?" This is quite peculiar, isn't it? If Lincoln had been the son of Tom Lincoln, would not Tom's father have been his grandfather? And do sensible people think for a moment that Abraham Lincoln had not heard the name of Tom's father mentioned? This is absurd! But Lincoln knew that Tom's father was not his grandfather, for Tom was not his father! That is what Abraham Lincoln meant, nothing else. But he really did not have the information as to who was his own grandfather on his real father's or mother's side. And this is his meaning.

Again, the worst blunder the Doctor made was in his statement as to what caused the death of Nancy Hanks, Lincoln's mother. "That she died of heart trouble from slanderous statements about her and old Abe Enloe" was an alarming statement.

Mr. Arthur, in his splendid *History of Western North Carolina*, brought this "suppressed" part of this old Doctor's story from its secret hiding place. He accuses Miss Tarbell of "suppressing" important matter which strongly corroborated the North Carolina history of Lincoln's origin. Arthur claimed that he had "great trouble in being able to secure this old Doctor's full statement," and "when he did, Lo, it had been 'garbled' and mutilated"!

Gossip About the Cause of Nancy's Death

Now, here is the special point for which I've quoted the full text of this old Doctor's statements though long they are. This statement about the death of Nancy takes the lid off and gives us a full view of the cross section of this poor woman's life. She was doubtless frequently reminded by Tom of her "mistakes" of former days before she came to Kentucky, though Tom knew all this when he married this girl, far his superior.

And this reference to the community psychology would hardly have held so many sharp teeth but for the fact that this so strongly corroborated all the other old stories, reaching clear back to North Carolina where Nancy had spent several years in this Enloe's home.

The unpleasant gossip was not about the "young Enloe" by the name of "Abraham" who lived in the Lincoln community as a "neighbor boy" upon whom late historians have spent so much time in trying to prove "he was not the father of Abraham Lincoln." This Kentucky Enloe is a young man, not over thirty-four years old when Nancy Hanks Lincoln died. And Tom never had any fight with Kentucky Enloe.

But at this time there was an "old Abe Enloe" with whom Tom's wife had lived in the State of North Carolina who was known to be the father of Nancy's boy "Abe"; and with whom Tom Lincoln had a terrible fight over Tom's whipping little Abe and Nancy so "brutally."

And this "old Abe Enloe" had paid Tom Lincoln "a mare and mule and money" for marrying Nancy and caring for the boy (Rev. Kennedy's story in this book; B. H. Melton; and Lamon's history). And this North Carolina Enloe was an "old man" at the time of Nancy's death.

The historians have found great difficulty in getting all these stubborn stories "sworn" out of existence. Dr. Barton's "spade" was so worn when he came across this affidavit that he did not try to "bury" this one. It, like many others, showed its sharp teeth and refused to be buried; and others though buried for a little while soon scratched their way out of their shallow graves.

If this gossip about Nancy's death had had no tentacles it could be more easily dealt with. But there is Judge Gilmore who lived near Fort Worth, Texas, who claimed that he knew Lincoln's mother before she married Tom Lincoln, and she then had a little boy called "Abe"; and that they played together and attended the same school in Kentucky (J. A. Collins). And there is the biting story by Attorney C. A. Ragland of Stockton, Missouri, who relates a conversation he had with Col. T. G. C. Davis, who had a law office in St. Louis. This Col. Davis was a cousin of Jeff Davis, President of the Confederacy. He was intimately acquainted with President Lincoln, having often been associated with him in law cases before the Supreme Court of Illinois, and they worked together as members of the same committee in drafting the constitution at a Constitutional Convention of Illinois.

Col. Davis claimed that he "knew the mother of Lincoln; that he was raised in the same neighborhood in Kentucky, and that it was generally understood, without question, in that neighborhood that Lincoln, the man who married the President's mother, was not the father of the President, but that his father's name was

Enloe" (J.C. Coggins, *Abraham Lincoln, a North Carolinian*, pp. 367; Hon. J.H. Cathey, *Truth Stranger Than Fiction*, p. 78; and Ragland's story in this book). And Lincoln tells a Mr. Davis, who is ready to "return to his old North Carolina home at Rutherfordton, N. C," that his mother was from there, and that his "right name" was Enloe, but that he had always gone by the name of his step-father (Cathey, p. 86).

Now, in view of these corroborating stories, one can see the probability of a foundation for what the old Doctor swore in regard to the community gossip about the death of Abraham Lincoln's mother. The background is sufficient to justify just such a situation when the jealousy of Tom Lincoln is taken into consideration.

Also, the "secret understanding between little Abe and his mother" will lend some weight in support of this theory (Ludwig).

This old Doctor, who seemed to be so thoroughly informed upon all matters of the community, said nothing about Nancy dying of "milk sickness" and being a physician it seems that it would have been in keeping with his profession to tell what it was that killed Lincoln's mother! But, instead, he goes on to relate what the historians didn't want told, "that some said she died of heart trouble, from slanders about her and old Abe Enloe, called Inlow, while her Abe, named for the pioneer Abraham Lincoln, was still little."

It has been contended by some that this unfortunate situation is what was the cause of changing the date of Lincoln's birth, and moving it up five years to incorporate this boy into Tom's own family to save embarrassment to the family, and more especially to Lincoln's mother. Of course it was a sad situation, and one over which the boy could have little control. But he had a great heart and was perfectly willing to suffer for his mother any kind of embarrassment if he could help to shield this, now, good mother from stinging tongues (Coleman).

But with a foundation laid in irrefutable fact it is impossible to control such a situation. So, it was talked everywhere this family lived; and it furnished no little influence in causing this family to migrate so frequently from place to place, apparently without any sufficient reason (Senator Beverage).

It is highly possible that this above statement as to the community gossip was true; that the neighbors did talk about the cause of Nancy's death; and that they had some foundation for saying "she died from heart trouble" caused by such reports.

I cannot believe the Kentucky people would manufacture willful lies about people after such a fashion. This is too villainous to be believed, even the devils in hell could be no less depraved!

But the people had eyes; they could see that this boy of Nancy's was not Tom's boy. No one of good judgment would have taken him for a "Lincoln." There were not any characteristics of Tom showing in this boy who was of a superior ancestry. People can detect the difference in stock instantly, and why not among people.

This boy was a perfect picture of Abraham Enloe, who moved to the mountains from Rutherford County in 1803 or 1804 (Col. Albert Logan in *The Vindicator*). And from this man's strong intellect and "extraordinary" personality this boy inherited a similar personality and a foundation for his future greatness (William H. Conley, et al).

CHAPTER TWENTY-ONE

Robert Lincoln's Inherited Mental Qualities

Lending weight to our position that it is impossible for a man of superior intellect to come from an ancestor of inferior or "subnormal mentality," we will now devote some time to the consideration of Mr. Robert Todd Lincoln, son of Abraham Lincoln.

This was the only child to live and have an opportunity to display the peculiar ancestral traits found in Abraham Lincoln. Robert Todd, eldest child of Abraham and Mary Todd Lincoln, was born in 1843, and died, I think, in 1926.

Both of these parents were people of superior intellect and good, substantial character, first-class American citizens, and it is very much to be regretted that they were not able to rear a large family. For here lies the only dependable foundation for a superior citizenship, in good ancestry. And this son never married, but lived the life of a hermit socially, for he was not a man who enjoyed society. And it may be that there was some reason for this apparently unnatural trait in this very strong-minded man. This may appear later.

Now, it was impossible for this son to have anything in his composition except what he inherited from his father and mother. He could not originate any part of himself. His mentality and his personality were the result of seed which could not produce anything else than it did produce. This law is just as inflexible as that for the production of vegetables, grain, or fowls, or animals of any kind. The quality and nature of the seed controls the life and largely predetermines the destiny.

And the great importance of securing the very best quality of seed corn, seed wheat, seed potatoes or of securing the highest and best breed of hogs, cattle or sheep, becomes very insignificant when compared to the seed for a higher type of citizen! This most important of all crops has been left to grow by "chance," until this country is fast becoming flooded with an inferior mentality; a degenerating class which is growing to such an alarming extent that it is now our country's greatest menace.

This young man, Robert Lincoln, inherited those sterling and outstanding mental qualities which so phenomenally distinguished his father.

1. First, he was a great student. He had an inborn relish for worth-while books to read and study. He was a boy who thought deeply and profoundly about things. His young soul, like that of his father, looked upward toward the mountain tops of knowledge and information; and now with his father's help, he is able to secure what was then impossible for the father – a college education. He graduated at Harvard University and Harvard Law School; and in 1864 he served on the staff of General Grant, and was admitted to the Chicago Bar in 1867. He practiced law in Chicago till in 1881.

2. His strong, logical mind led him, as did the mind of the father, to the study and practice of the law. And soon the extra quality of mind and character are so pronounced in this young man as to attract attention. Had he been of scrub, or of a low-class, of stock he would have attracted no attention. But he is not of the "Tom Lincoln" stock! And consequently, this man is not going to stop where the Tom Lincoln family left off.

3. As the people "looked up to" and came for advice and council to both his father, and the grandfather, Abraham Enloe, so now they feel the need of this man's wise council, where he served

THE EUGENICS OF PRESIDENT ABRAHAM LINCOLN 177

as Secretary of War in the Cabinets of Presidents Garfield and Arthur, from 1881 to 1885. And then he served his country as Minister to Great Britain from 1889 to 1893. Here were displayed those excellent qualities of mind and heart found in his father and grandfather, of honesty, sobriety and integrity of character, making him capable, dependable and trustworthy in office.

And while the "business qualities" were not so pronounced in his father, Abraham Lincoln, as they were in his grandfather, Abraham Enloe of North Carolina, this young man has inherited sterling business sense. It was said that Abraham Enloe, his real grandfather, "was an excellent business man" (H.J. Beck). Since there is always a great demand for such rare talent, in 1897, Robert Lincoln became the President of the Pullman Car Company of Chicago, and in 1911 was made the Chairman of its board of directors. These positions he held till his death.

Thus, by that inborn, persistent pluck, push, and intrinsic worth of personality, this man just grew into positions of honor and great responsibility, until he became a man of wealth. "He was a good business man."

A Strange Thing Robert Lincoln's Will

There was something strange in the will of the late Robert Lincoln – something which aroused a profound interest throughout the entire country. The announcement in the papers became an insolvable riddle to the people, and they were wondering and talking everywhere about a strange item mentioned as a "codicil" to Robert Lincoln's will.

The last part of this man's testament stated that "there was a little private box of his father's papers, of a personal character, which he wished and willed should not be opened or disturbed for twenty years"! And the people were amazed at such a startling announcement.

Why are the people not allowed to know the contents of this little "box" now? If the people should ever be allowed to know the contents, why keep them in suspense? What could be gained by such a postponement? These are some of the questions the people have been asking ever since the death of Robert Lincoln.

There appears to be but one answer to these questions.

This little mysterious box contains the solution of the "Lincoln mystery," about which historians and writers have had so much to say for over a hundred years: Abraham Lincoln wants the people to know one truth, the real facts about his origin! He knew they wanted to know this, and he will tell them!

But there were some people, yet living, who had taken this matter to heart, and who were so sensitive upon this question of Lincoln's "illegitimacy" that Lincoln preferred not to disillusion these good old "friends" of former years. This would have been a very severe shock to those old people! And to save their feelings he had the time for opening this box and telling the whole world the simple truth, postponed till after they were gone! There can be no other solution. This is in perfect harmony with the entire life-story of Abraham Lincoln.

And when the twenty years are up, the time specified in the will for the opening of this box, in about 1946, Abraham Lincoln will speak to the American people again about his ancestry.

He told James Speed that he did not know who his grandfather was. But that he, himself, was more interested in what the grandson would become! He told, in great confidence, that his right name was Enloe, but that he had always gone by the name of his step-father.

He stated at Cooper Institute, New York, that he was not related to the "Benjamine Lincoln" of Massachusetts, as has been claimed. He knew he was not a Lincoln.

He had appointed to office during his Presidency, two of his close Enloe relatives, though they were Democrats in principle (Attorney J.S. Styles of Asheville).

Robert Knows The Story

And this story was no secret to Abraham Lincoln's son.

He knew his ancestry. He knew he was not akin to the Lincolns; that "there was not a drop of Lincoln blood in him." And, feeling his better blood, he was proud, in a manner, for there was good stock on both sides running back to England and Germany from which developed strong, virulent leaders, scholars, school men, physicians, jurists, statesmen, and business men of very high quality.

But the people called him a "hermit," a "recluse," and wondered why such a man should not regale himself with a delightful social life which was always open to such a man of wealth and position. But having learned in the early histories, as well as the recent publications and from his father, that he was wearing the wrong name and that there were many people who knew this to be true, he, like his father, felt at times the pain of an inward "cancer"; yes, this good man, too, felt the sting of his great father's "illegitimacy"! Robert knew this to be true! There had been brought to him ample proof of this fact.

People for a long time had been asking the pertinent question, and they came to me about it, saying, "Why doesn't Robert Lincoln sue the people for slander or libel, those who dare to blacken the reputation of his father?" I replied, "Robert knows all about it!"

Robert was, like his father, a good lawyer, and he knew the law. But knowing the facts about his father's origin, he was disarmed for any defense and had no statements whatever to make. And this had an influence upon this son, to house himself in, to wall himself in from the social world; to make of himself a "hermit."

CHAPTER TWENTY-TWO

The Evidence "Under Lock And Key"

It has been positively asserted that Abraham Lincoln's law partner and first historian, William Herndon, held in his possession a large collection of manuscripts and notations bearing upon the question of Lincoln's illegitimacy. Evidently such information was the basis upon which he made such strong statements in the first edition of his book, the three volume edition, which it is claimed has been "suppressed" for this reason.

And it is claimed that Mr. Herndon before his death "receded" from his former belief based upon these old manuscripts (Barton, p. 306). Though there was one particular reason that was never published, containing a specific time and place limitation, in Herndon's possession, and since Herndon's death has, with other valuable manuscripts, been kept securely under lock and key in a fire-proof building.

Dr. Barton makes mention of this "unpublished reason" among these old papers and notes of the first historian as having caused Mr. Herndon to "affirm with the greatest confidence" that Lincoln was, as claimed by many, an "illegitimate." It was only a matter of guess or conjecture as to where Herndon had received this evidence, which to this lawyer (Herndon) was of such tremendous weight. It seemed to offer a different kind of argument from all other documents in its "time and place limitations."

The Rosetta Stone

Here is a kind of "key" to this mysterious situation: a kind of "Rosetta Stone," from which it is possible to secure valuable information if one is able to translate its peculiar inscriptions.

And we believe we can translate this piece of hieroglyphics to the satisfaction of any careful reader. There are only two specifications included: time and place.

It will be noted that persistent and strenuous efforts have been made to fence in this boy, Abraham Lincoln, so that he would be born on the right side of the marriage ceremony of Tom and Nancy. Now, if they can just arrange to have him born at Elizabethtown, or Hodgensville, at the proper time after the wedding, he will belong to Tom whether he bears any resemblance or not. And to prove this has been the burden of historians.

But if he were actually born before this wedding, as often "asserted" by many, and in another State before his mother became acquainted with Tom Lincoln, then he was not Tom's boy!

This will meet the time and place specifications. And we have already proven by evidence sufficiently strong to make out a case in court, before any impartial jury that this girl Nancy Hanks lived in the home of Abraham Enloe of North Carolina; and that she was driven from the Enloe home by Mrs. Enloe under an unfavorable situation in which Mrs. Enloe implicated her husband; and that after Nancy's child was born in Rutherford County, North Carolina, she, with the child, was sent to Kentucky; and after residing in Kentucky for some time she was married to Thomas Lincoln; and that this marriage involved a monetary consideration from Abraham Enloe with whom this girl had lived in North Carolina; and that Tom was abusive to this mother and child, precipitating a terrible battle between Enloe and Lincoln; that these parties made friends and the Lincolns came back to North Carolina upon a visit, to Abraham Enloe and while there

Enloe gave Tom Lincoln a mare and a mule and money as a payment on the sum promised for marrying this girl with the child "Abraham." And highly corroborative of all this chain of evidence offered thus far are the independent Tennessee stories, one of which has come from a member of Tom Lincoln's family, stating that Tom Lincoln and his wife and child went on horseback from Abraham Enloe's to visit Tom's uncle Isaac at Elizabethton, Tennessee, where they remained for some time (J. D. Jenkins); and that on their way back to Kentucky Tom's wife was employed as cook at a logging camp at Rutlege, Tennessee; and that this furnishes a solution for the "mystery" as to where Tom Lincoln got the money with which to make the payment on the 300-acre farm he purchased about this time.

It would be utterly impossible for a story to be so perfectly articulated as this is putting together independent stories, unless it had a foundation in truth. So the old manuscript under lock and key, which led William Herndon to believe in Lincoln's illegitimacy, supports our theory. And if Mr. Herndon did "recede" from this view in later years as claimed by Dr. Barton, it was not for lack of evidence to sustain what he and others had claimed, but it was rather the abuse to which this man was constantly subjected for making this public.

Such tirades of abuse from the pulpit by ministers of the gospel, even from the church (Presbyterian) attended by Mr. Herndon's family, have rarely ever been equaled in epithets and vituperation, as were turned loose upon this historian and friend of Lincoln. It was a very shameful procedure by people who thought they were doing Mr. Lincoln an honor, but were mistaken. They dishonored the truth!

CHAPTER TWENTY-THREE

Was Herndon, Lincoln's Partner, a Judas?

Various apologists and writers on Lincoln biography have gone so far as to class William Herndon as an "enemy" of Abraham Lincoln. And because of this fact, we deem it proper at this point to go into this question at considerable length as it is claimed Herndon "hatched up all these false rumors." And they claim that Herndon then turned his material all over to Mr. Lamon, the next historian, who was almost as bad as Herndon.

As no building can be more substantial than its foundation, or no case in court can be more invulnerable than the basic evidence upon which the case rests, it is important that we go into this matter and make an examination of its contents.

We shall put upon the witness stand at least two capable and reliable witnesses who are conversant with the situation on both sides, and who are friends of President Lincoln, and see what these witnesses of good standing have to say of William Herndon and his attitude toward Mr. Lincoln.

William Herndon is indicted for slandering the good name of Abraham Lincoln, on trial by "the Presbyterian preacher, Rev. James A. Reed, pastor of the First Presbyterian Church, Springfield."

This preacher turned his artillery with the force of a wild Texas tornado on this first historian, leaving neither "hair nor hoof" when he had finished his lambastic "lecture." This indictment of Mr. Herndon was published in *Scribner's Monthly* in 1873, and delivered to a number of large audiences in Northern cities, to the great delight of the listeners.

In this public arraignment, Herndon was held up before the people as the villain, the betrayer, the Judas Iscariot, the drunken galout, the apostate and infidel slanderer of the name of his former friend and benefactor, Abraham Lincoln.

This serious charge by this popular man "of the cloth" was not publicly answered by the historian. He was then an old man, and with little money; and the bitter feeling engendered by such charges rendered him exceedingly unpopular.

If the other side could have been heard at that time; if some man as capable as the Presbyterian minister could have taken the "old manuscripts," confidential letters and "records" then in the possession of William Herndon, and with these made a defense of this poor old "preacher-cussed" lawyer, the case would now read differently!

But, as the boy said, "they had 'em stood!" There was no one to volunteer and come to the defense of "the old infidel." He was now, in the eyes of the people, "down and out!"

But as time passes the people, more calmly weighing the matter, could see that all this effusive bombast and vitriolic villificating were not argument! This hot blast was not founded upon facts in contradiction of Herndon. He did not prove Mr. Herndon a liar! He only said so.

And it is due the people as well as Mr. Herndon to furnish the proof in refutation of what Mr. Herndon and others had stated. But it turns out that this rebuttal is lacking in evidence.

Another important point which should not be overlooked is, that while Dr. Barton, a kind of prosecutor and persecutor of Herndon who claims that Herndon "receded" from his former belief in Lincoln's illegitimacy, he submits no proof of such recession, either of his own or of William Herndon's! He writes down a simple statement that the historian said, "It is still charged that Abraham Lincoln was the son of one Enloe." "My own opinion, after a searching examination, is that Mrs. Lincoln [Nancy Hanks] was not a bad woman; was by nature a noble woman. My own opinion is that Abraham Lincoln is the son and heir of Thomas Lincoln and Nancy Hanks Lincoln."

Well, from a legal viewpoint, as this had been stated in the family, it was in law true that he was heir, but not in fact!

But as there are not any dates given for this supposed change in the belief of Mr. Herndon, Mr. Barton could not say with any degree of certainty just when this supposed statement was made. He thinks it was made after the strong statement to the contrary, in the "wonderful document" written by Herndon in proof of Lincoln's illegitimacy, and which had "never been made public"; but which had caused Herndon to "affirm with the greatest confidence" that Abraham Lincoln was not the son of Tom Lincoln (Barton, p. 306).

Now if something had been found after this time which proved to Herndon that his belief was unfounded, it should be given to the people showing that the historian had found new evidence in the case. And then this new evidence could cause this "case" which had been settled in the mind of the historian to be reopened for another "trial." But nothing further is given by Mr. Herndon, Dr. Barton or any one else. And hence it really is, in law, settled, *"res adjudicata!"*

Witnesses For The Plaintiff – Herndon

We are unwilling for the "accused," Herndon, Lamon, et al, to be condemned to everlasting ignominy without some semblance of defense. This is unAmerican and unfair. The low-grade of Negroes who so forgot themselves as to commit rape upon White women in Alabama have been shown far more consideration than have these "accused" White men! Northern men and money have been able to "continue and re-continue, and appeal and re-appeal" this Scotsborough Case for many years in the most flagrant violation of justice and of decency.

The first witness we offer is the Hon. Judge G. W. Murray of Springfield, Illinois, who gave this statement to Rev. William E. Barton, D.D., April 21, 1920, as follows:

> I was partner of William H. Herndon in this city in the year 1878. I had come in 1876 from Ohio, my native State. I was born near Troy, Ohio in July, 1839, and shall be on my next birthday. I was elected Judge in 1890, and served continuously, excepting between 1894 and 1898, when I was not on the bench. My whole term of service as Judge was sixteen years.
>
> I came to Illinois with great admiration for Abraham Lincoln, and was glad to be associated with a man who had known him intimately as Mr. Herndon had known him. Mr. Herndon was as willing to talk about Lincoln as I was to listen.
>
> Continuously, when we were not busy and perhaps at some times when we should have been at work, he talked to me of Lincoln. There was hardly any period of Lincoln's life, or phase of his character, we did not discuss.
>
> It had been charged that Mr. Herndon was embittered against Mr. Lincoln, and a reason has been assigned in Mr. Lincoln's alleged refusal to give Mr. Herndon an office which Mr. Herndon is alleged to have coveted. I believe this to be untrue, both as to the fact and as to the motive. So far from Mr. Herndon's cherishing resentment against Mr. Lincoln, the whole character of his conversations, which were many, discredits that statement. I can remember no single word spoken by him concerning Mr. Lincoln in which there appeared to be any such animus. He held Lincoln in the highest admiration. He had no regrets for any thing that had ever occurred between them.
>
> Mr. Herndon told me that Mr. Lincoln offered him office. My impression is that there was more than one such offer. One that I remember was of a judicial character, a position in what I think was called the Court of Claims, a Court established to consider claims of Southern people against the Government for damages alleged to have been suffered by them during the war. He spoke of other positions which he believed he might have had. He said that he did not desire office.

There is absolutely nothing in the charge that Mr. Herndon cherished any spirit of unfriendliness toward Mr. Lincoln, or any feeling of disappointment because of his failure to secure through Mr. Lincoln political appointment.

Toward Mrs. Lincoln, Herndon had no kindly feelings. He did not denounce her, nor refer to her in terms which a gentleman might not with propriety use toward a lady, but he did not like her, and she did not like him; and he believed that she made Mr. Lincoln's home life unhappy. He believed that Mr. Lincoln had loved Ann Rutledge, and that her memory was very dear to him.

Mr. Herndon continually spoke of Mr. Lincoln's greatness and goodness. He told me of traveling over the State from one county seat to another with the meager law-library in saddlebags. Often Lincoln went to a session of Court without any client, but he almost always secured clients on the ground through his association with local attorneys. Herndon spoke of Lincoln's ability as a lawyer and statesman. He also admired greatly Lincoln's kindness of heart, his forgiving disposition. He was greatly impressed by Mr. Lincoln's attitude of kindness toward young men in the army who were found guilty of transgression of military regulations.

His habitual attitude toward the memory of Lincoln was one of admiration.

In short, I cannot remember a single instance in which he spoke unkindly of Lincoln, but invariably the reverse. I was a warm admirer of Abraham Lincoln before I became Herndon's partner; but under the influence of Herndon that admiration grew to a sincere affection and devotion.

Largely through what Mr. Herndon related to me, I have spoken from time to time about Mr. Lincoln in public addresses, one of which I delivered at the Lincoln monument in this city in 1903, and another before the Author's Club in 1913. The sincere admiration which in these and other addresses I have invariably expressed for Abraham Lincoln is in full accord with the spirit in which Mr. Herndon spoke of him.

It has been charged that Mr. Herndon believed and charged that Abraham Lincoln was an illegitimate child. I know what Herndon wrote, which has been thus construed, and in my judgment Mr. Herndon did not intend to convey that impression. I believe that Herndon believed that Lincoln was of legitimate birth, and would have resented a charge to the contrary. I knew Mr. Herndon too intimately and talked with him too freely to be mistaken about his real feeling toward Mr. Lincoln. He honored Lincoln and I learned in association with Herndon to honor more and more the character of Abraham Lincoln.

(Signed) G. W. Murray
April 21st, 1920

Now, since the strength of any case depends altogether upon the character of the witnesses and the strength of the testimony they furnish, it will be seen that the above testimony of Judge Murray is first-class. In fact there can be no better witness as to whether Herndon was an "enemy" of Lincoln. And we submit that any reasonable, unprejudiced man will be willing to accept this as proof of our contention in defense of Mr. Herndon. Herndon, like many people, had his weaknesses, but yet he was a good man, and a "devoted" friend of President Lincoln. He was offered a judgeship, an honorable and paying position under Lincoln, but declined this splendid offer preferring to remain "Lincoln's law partner," in the office at home. And this partnership only terminated at the tragic death of Mr. Lincoln.

In addition to the above statement from Judge Murray, we will add a word from Mr. Herndon's family. It is but proper, since Mr. Herndon has been charged as being a bitter enemy of Abraham Lincoln, that we let Herndon's daughters have a word to say in their father's defense. This would be allowed in court. Though their testimony cannot have the weight that Judge Murray's has because of their personal interest in the case, yet it will deserve due consideration.

Mrs. Annie Fleury, the eldest daughter of Mr. Herndon, after a statement in her father's defense as to being a real "infidel" and how he saw God in all the manifold forms of creation everywhere, in the birds, flowers, trees and rippling brooks (though not a man of manufactured creeds he was a believer in God), remembered how he joked with his children:

> He was always teasing his daughters. When he came home from the office he would ask me, "Who was that dirty-faced little boy I saw kissing you through the fence?" He was delighted with my indignant denials, and would catch me up and laugh heartily at my loudly proclaimed innocence. When he was through with his teasing, he would romp with us, and instruct us. He was a loving father. He was not "orthodox," and was much opposed to the theology of his time. I think if he were living now he would not be thought of as an infidel. He had his faults and his weaknesses; and his children have some memories that are not happy ones. But he was an honest man, an intelligent man, a man who loved freedom and God and his children and Mr. Lincoln.

I feel confident the foregoing testimony will, clear Mr. Herndon of the aspersions which some historians have cast upon him for what he has written in his first history of Abraham Lincoln, published in three volumes, and from which a number of quotations have been made in this book. I think all such calumnious remarks about Mr. Herndon were unjustified and were made only because of certain things Herndon told, in his history, that some people wished he had "consigned to the tomb." But Herndon thought these things were necessary for the people to know in order for them to know Lincoln! In this edition, Herndon says:

> If the story of his life is truthfully and courageously told, nothing colored or suppressed, nothing false either written or suggested, the reader will see and feel the real presence of the man.
> If on the other hand, the story is colored, or the facts in any degree suppressed, the reader will be not only misled, but imposed upon as well. At last the truth will come and no man need hope to evade it.
> Lincoln's character I am certain will bear a close scrutiny. I am not afraid of you in this direction. Don't let anything deter you from digging to the bottom. In drawing the portrait, tell the world what the "skeleton" was with Lincoln. What gave him

that peculiar melancholy. What cancer had he inside. Especial attention is given to the history of his youth and early manhood, and while dwelling on this portion of his life, the liberty is taken to insert many things that would be omitted or suppressed in other places where the cast-iron rules that govern magazine writing prevail.

Mr. Lincoln was my warm, devoted friend. I always loved him, and revere his name today.

My purpose to tell the truth about him need occasion no apprehension, for I know that God's naked truth, as Carlyle puts it, can never injure the fame of Abraham Lincoln.

Some persons will doubtless object to the narrative of certain facts, which appear here for the first time, and which they contend should be consigned to the tomb. Their pretense is that no good can come from such ghastly exposures. To such over-sensitive souls, if any such exist, my answer is that these facts are indispensable to a full knowledge of Mr. Lincoln in all the walks of life (Herndon and Weik).

The above is the unwhitewashed statement of an honest man who felt it his duty to tell the truth about Lincoln's origin. And while he was Mr. Lincoln's "devoted friend," he felt that a great injustice would be done to the reader of history if these things were omitted. The reader would be misled and imposed upon! And the real truth would come anyway and no man could evade it.

Now, if these things were the truth, why slaughter this historian for "courageously" telling what he had found to be the truth? This is very wrong! It is just as culpable as participating in the slave trade. With the indisputable facts in Herndon's possession, he felt that he would be an unmitigated liar to palm off this intellectual giant, whom he loved as the son of the intellectually "subnormal" Tom Lincoln! (Senator Beverage). And Herndon was right! He wanted the people to know what that "skeleton" was; what caused the "melancholy; what lay back of that great "sad face": what it was that caused Lincoln to think of committing suicide; and why he would steal away from the stirring crowds of people and bury himself in the wilderness, far away from the people, in deep meditation.

Herndon was a classical scholar, a well educated gentleman who could write well, much better than some of his traducers and would-be critics; and he certainly must have been well fortified in the position he held in regard to Mr. Lincoln.

Now, when we seriously consider the statements made by another very able lawyer and Supreme Court Judge of the State of Kentucky, we find the most astonishing corroboration. And inasmuch as we have cleared Mr. Herndon of the charge of being Mr. Lincoln's "enemy," we will now support him with independent testimony.

Judge Peters' Affidavit

The following story, said to be the most widely circulated story in Kentucky in regard to Lincoln's illegitimacy, strongly corroborates what Herndon says, and indirectly helps to clear Mr. Herndon of the harsh charges made against him at Springfield by the preacher.

> I was graduated from Transylvania University, Kentucky, in 1825. I read law with John Boyle, Chief Justice of Kentucky; I obtained license to practice law in 1827. My legal and professional career has extended over a period of over sixty years. In all that time I have never heard, among my legal friends (and I have known nearly all the lawyers, old and young, in the State) the fact of Abraham Lincoln's illegitimacy disputed.

It is said that this story is "very widely circulated" and in one of its forms it declares that "Jesse Head, when a resident of Harrodsburg, Kentucky, told an eminent lawyer that Abraham Lincoln was born and old enough to be running around at the time when he married Thomas Lincoln to Nancy Hanks."

Judge Peters wrote this story for the local papers in his home town, Mount Sterling, and toward the end of his life he took occasion to make oath to his belief in the truth of this story.

A sketch of Judge Peter's life is in a book, entitled *The Bench and Bar of Kentucky*, showing him to be a man of the highest reputation for truth and veracity.

From the fact that he published this in the papers, probably when Abraham Lincoln was making his campaign with Douglas, as other papers were asking "Who is this man Lincoln?" at this time, is strong presumptive evidence he then had the proof in his possession. And the strange thing seems to be that there was not any answer of correction to the newspaper reports claiming that "he was the son of an Abraham Enloe of Western North Carolina!" (Cathey, and this author's book *Abraham Lincoln, a North Carolinian*, pp. 138-139).

There should have been some answer then! And not wait 75 years, till all the evidence has been destroyed and the witnesses all dead who knew these things to be true. Such procedure is taking undue advantage of the facts in the case.

Now, when we consider the consistency, the correlation, the corroboration of all these independent stories, one with another, their articulation, the idea of fraud, collusion, or any kind of conspiracy is absolutely unreasonable and out of the question. And his first biographer, William Herndon, stands unimpeached!

Mr. Ward Lamon

Mr. Ward Hill Lamon, who bought the Herndon Manuscript at $2,000.00, can be and has been placed in the same category with Mr. Herndon as "an enemy of Abraham Lincoln." This man was President Lincoln's body-guard in times of greatest peril. He loved and honored Lincoln as but few people did. Yet this man has been covered with the spittle and mud of apologists till he would be hardly recognized. And all because, like poor old Herndon, he wanted to tell the people the truth instead of lies.

And these oldest and best historians of Lincoln will "rise from the dead," doubtless in the year 1946, when the little box is opened! The opening of this box will be the opening of their graves as truth-loving and truth-telling historians! Then they will be fully vindicated, after having been ostracized, abused, and exiled for a great number of years.

CHAPTER TWENTY-FOUR

☆ ☆ ☆ ☆

Little Abraham Rides Between Thomas And Nancy

There is no story more extensively told in Kentucky than this, about "little Abraham riding away from the wedding between his mother and Thomas Lincoln." And though this was not incorporated in the affidavit of Chief Justice Peters, yet it was a part of the story upon which was based his affidavit. This was believed by almost everybody, including all the lawyers of the State. And when this story is so strongly supported by the various other data bearing upon this intricate question it becomes very much more credible (Barton, p. 72).

And this story is strongly corroborated by the number of good people who say they saw this child of Nancy Hanks in the home of Richard Berry, where the parents were married, and also that his name was on a tax return, supposed to be 1811, though it is not on this list now! Mr. Polin, County Attorney, thinks the tax list which contained the names of Tom's children was 1809, as the population tallied with this date, and did not tally with the year 1811.

To keep little Abraham in the fold, Dr. Barton would have Tom Lincoln "move back to Washington County and live about a year there before moving to Indiana." Little Abe has been seen running around there at the "Berry's" by a number of people, corroborating the Justice Peters' story that he was there at the wedding; and Dr. Barton proposes to build a new fence around this boy; he has to be kept with Tom's family. It is very dangerous for him to wander off from Tom's family. Judge Gilmore, of Fort Worth, Texas, had seen him, off by himself, before his mother married Tom Lincoln. But this has to be fixed by the Rev. Dr. Barton. Of course, it is not wrong to "make up" a little history to take care of a fine boy like this! Though of course the accepted version is that the family moved directly to Indiana from Knob Creek.

CHAPTER TWENTY-FIVE

Res Adjudicata – The "Fixed Date"

While the apologists have tried hard to persuade the people to believe that the date February 12, 1809 is a "fixed date" and definitely stands as an impregnable Gibraltar against all adverse criticism, yet a careful analysis of this question will undoubtedly reveal some very weak spots. We have already shown a suitable reason, as to why it could have been possible to set this up as a fictitious date for Mr. Lincoln's birth. That under the embarrassing circumstances, to be successful, it was the only thing he could do! And the record confirms us in the belief that Mr. Lincoln was a man of great political ambition.

This record of his "birthday" was not "fixed" by Lincoln's mother nor by Tom Lincoln, nor by anyone else who had any correct idea as to the exact time and place of his birth. And as for his own "personal knowledge," he could not have known anything about the time and place! No child knows the time and place of its birth!

We have already shown that there was one of two good reasons which might have influenced him in this camouflage: one purely political and the other "to shield his mother from scandal," as has been suggested (Coleman).

It is rather peculiar that Lincoln is the one who "fixed" this date. This shows on the family Bible; but there is no way of telling the time when this entry was made. He probably made his step-mother a present of a family Bible, after he had entered the political arena after he was in Congress, at which time the pot began to boil stronger about his "illegitimacy." And when at home on a visit, he and she, Mrs. Sarah Bush Lincoln, probably "fixed" this matter. This was all the "record" available, aside from a letter from Mr. Lincoln in 1843, in which he says, "he was born in 1809."

This first date-fixing letter of Lincoln, written in 1848, saying, "I am now in my fortieth year," was after his entrance into politics. It seems very strange that there could not be found an earlier record anywhere! Add this "fortieth" year to his birthday, "1809," and it would make this declaration to have occurred in 1849, over a decade after he had entered into political campaigns, and had been defeated in his race for the State Legislature in 1832, and was elected to this office in 1834, serving until 1842, when he declined further nomination. Then he made another statement in 1860, saying he was born in 1809. And the sketches that he prepared for his campaign biographers, Fell, Scripps, and Hicks, in 1859 and 1860, are made to correspond with the date mentioned by him in 1848, when he was "in his fortieth year."

To suggest that this was done as a political expedient probably gets nearer the truth than any other surmise. By this time this man was "constantly receiving letters in regard to his illegitimacy," says his partner, Herndon, and "which Lincoln never answered."

Here that "cancer," mentioned by Mr. Herndon, begins to grow, and Lincoln did all he could to stop its growth before it would kill him, politically. He announced the false date, making himself the legitimate son of Thomas Lincoln and Nancy Hanks Lincoln.

Mr. Lincoln was elected to Congress in 1846, and grew from then on to his Presidency in 1861.

It would thus appear that "the Bible record" in Lincoln's

handwriting, about which such strong claims for "fixedness" have been made by some historians, cannot of itself be very reassuring as this entry could not have been made before the death of Thomas Lincoln, whose death is recorded as having occurred January 15, 1851, having been born January 6, 1778.

Then, instead of this date being something "fixed" – to which everything else which appears in his boyhood experiences are forced to yield priority – is wrong. It is historical camouflage in the matured and professional writing of Abraham Lincoln.

Therefore, this matter which, as the lawyer would designate as *"res adjudicata,"* things adjudicated or settled, have not really been properly settled, and cannot be, when it can be clearly shown that this date is in irreconcilable conflict with all Lincoln's boyhood life, and the date 1812, when Lincoln, eight years old, was pulled out of Knob Creek by his schoolmate, Austin Gollaher. There must be harmony in history or it is not true history.

Abraham Lincoln said, "My right name is Enloe, but I have always gone by the name of my step-father" (Cathey, p. 86). In spite of all the "spades" and camouflage, this was a wrongly-named President.

Camping at Night in the Wilderness

There were at least three families who left Rutherford County together to make their homes in the mountains, and Nancy Hanks, the mother of Abraham Lincoln, was in the Enloe family making this journey. This was in the year 1803 or 1804. They built huge bonfires at night to keep off the wild animals, and some of the party would sit up and watch while the others slept in the wagons.

CHAPTER TWENTY-SIX

The Negro-Blood Story – A Malicious Slander

I have been requested by the State Historian of Virginia, Miss Mary D. Carter, to make some remarks in regard to the late rumor that has been circulated, to the effect that Lincoln was of Negro blood ancestry. I am told that this rumor was based upon the theory that his mother was from South Carolina, and that this has "right extensively circulated in some parts of the South."

This is an inexcusable injustice, based upon both ignorance and a long-standing sectional hatred of a great and good man. This story is absolutely without any foundation in fact. It is probably based upon the idea that there may have been some "mixed blood" in the South Carolina Nancy Hanks, though there is no proof of this.

While it has been alleged by some of the South Carolina people that Lincoln was the son of John C. Calhoun by the South Carolina "Nancy Hanks," this was impossible. For it is positively proven that this South Carolina Hanks family was not the family from which Abraham Lincoln sprang.

This South Carolina Nancy lived in the home of her own parents, Luke and Ann Hanks, till she was grown, when she became "entangled" with John C. Calhoun, it is said.

201

This tradition recites that "Calhoun hired Thomas Lincoln, who was working for Abraham Enloe to take the girl away, paying him $500.00."

This is untrue for the following reasons:

1. Thomas Lincoln never "worked for Abraham Enloe" unless it was the Kentucky Enloe, and there is no evidence of that.

2. Lincoln's mother was born in Virginia, and not in South Carolina.

3. The name of Lincoln's maternal grandmother was "Lucy Hanks," while the name of the South Carolina mother of that "Nancy" is "Ann."

4. Lincoln's mother was an "illegitimate" daughter of "Lucy Hanks and a Virginian of the best blood of the State," said President Lincoln to Herndon, the historian, and is so regarded by historians.

5. The name of the South Carolina girl's father was "Luke" Hanks.

6. Moreover, "Lucy" never married anyone by the name of "Luke."

7. Herndon declared that "Lucy Hanks had never been married before she married Henry Sparrow in Kentucky in...." If she had been married, it had been to the father of Nancy, Lincoln's mother, Mr. Michael Tanner of Virginia. This Tanner family kept the "records," proving that Michael was the father of Lincoln's mother, and that Michael and Lucy Hanks were married, and that "his wife Lucy died in childbirth, and the infant 'Nancy Hanks' was then given to Michael's brother Dan to raise with his children."

But there are too many weak places in this theory that Mr. Tanner, the real father of Nancy Hanks, had married Lucy. If this had been true she would have been kept in the Tanner family and would have worn the name "Tanner" instead of "Hanks." But the grandmother of Lincoln, "Lucy Hanks," did not "die in childbirth," and was well known in Rutherford County, North Carolina, and later in Kentucky, where she was married to Sparrow; and before her marriage she was "indicted for fornication," showing that she had been a woman of loose character.

8. Abraham Lincoln was already born and was two years old at the time they claimed a relation existed between Calhoun and the South Carolina Hanks girl. That was about 1807 or 1808, and we have submitted ample proof in this book that Lincoln was born before this time; the correct date probably being February 12, 1804.

9. This Abraham Enloe had this girl, after her child was born, taken to Kentucky, where he sent her money for the child's support (B.H. Melton).

10. It was told that he was to pay Tom Lincoln for marrying this girl "$500.00 and a wagon, and team."

11. This man Enloe engaged in a fight with Tom Lincoln for the "brutal abuse of this woman and child."

12. When Lincoln became President, people wrote from Rutherford County, where Nancy Hanks had lived in the former home of Enloe, asking if the President was the son of Nancy Hanks, who had formerly lived in Rutherford County, and the reply was "Yes, he is the son of the same Nancy Hanks who used to live in North Carolina" (J. H. Martin, a former Sheriff of Rutherford County, North Carolina).

13. This old letter had been seen by the old ex-Sheriff with whom I talked when I received this information.

14. This story corroborates the old document in the custody of a member of the Tanner family, saying that this North Carolina Nancy was the mother of the President.

15. Thomas Lincoln, with Nancy and little Abraham, made a visit to see Abraham Enloe, at Ocona Lufta, now near Bryson City, North Carolina, and stayed several days; and when they got ready to leave "Enloe gave Tom a mare and mule and money" (Rev. S.E. Kennedy and B.H. Melton).

16. When they returned to Kentucky, Tom sprang a great surprise upon his neighbors and the future historians by buying a fine farm, paying $200.00 cash down! And the historians are yet at a great loss to know "where Tom found all this money" without having to work for it like other folks. And it is claimed he then owned two horses at this same time! (Dr. Warren, pp. 54, 55).

CHAPTER TWENTY-SEVEN

Startling Testimony

Like very much valuable evidence which has been carelessly or purposely thrown into the trash pile, we have found the important and clinching statement of a daughter of John Hanks, bearing directly and convincingly upon the subject under discussion. We had never expected to ever be able to secure such conclusive testimony, from the other side, in this discussion.

Mrs. Manon, a daughter of John Hanks, residing in California, gives the most damaging testimony of any yet received. Her father was an associate of Abraham Lincoln for many years near Springfield, Illinois, and where this daughter of John Hanks also lived when she was a girl.

Her name was Mary Ellen Hanks, and she says she was about eighteen years old when Lincoln was nominated for the Presidency. She knew Lincoln well, and also Dennis Hanks, her father's cousin. She also was acquainted with the relatives, the four sisters of whom Dennis spoke, of whom one was "Lucy" the mother of Nancy Hanks, Lincoln's own mother. They all lived near Springfield. And "Lucy Hanks" was also the aunt of Thomas Lincoln.

This lady says: "Thomas and Nancy had one child, Sarah,

and their friends after Nancy's death tried to fix the records to date back the marriage, and failed signally" (Barton, p. 115).

Dr. Barton, knowing his "spade" would go to pieces upon coming in contact with this inflexible piece of evidence, quietly let it alone. It is very peculiar how such valuable statements, like great nuggets of gold or diamonds, have ruthlessly been walked over by some historians like prehistoric savages treading upon South African diamond fields.

Prof. Greenleaf, the great author of *A Treatise on the Law of Evidence*, says, "We should not only accept the testimony of good and reliable people, but we should accept the testimony of bad people when there appears to be no motive which they might have for telling anything but the truth."

Now, for all we know this is a good woman. But if she were not a good woman then it would have to be shown that she must have had some sinister motive in giving the testimony she did. For she, being related to the people on the other side, would not be expected to bear the strongest kind of testimony against them! And this she does. Therefore, it naturally follows, as the light follows the sun, that this woman was telling the simple truth about this case. She had no need to manufacture or change the story to pervert the truth. She could just as well have left this part out of the story. But she considered this very pertinent, which it was, to throw light upon this great mystery. And she turned on the light!

The Truth Comes Out

1. The first point we call attention to is the statement that Tom and Nancy had but one child, a girl named "Sarah," This unlocks a little musty dungeon and lets the light shine in. There has been all kinds of speculation about this girl, the apologists claiming she was older than Abraham Lincoln, and affidavits had to be fixed up to prove this for the old people didn't believe it. They all understood the situation just like this girl who tells the truth about it.

This lady who was a girl back there in the family of John Hanks is the very highest authority. She not only shows that Abraham Lincoln was not the son of Tom Lincoln at all, corroborating all our other independent testimony upon this subject, but that he was born before the marriage of Tom and Nancy, and for this reason the "friends after his mother's death" tried to fence him in with Tom's family and "signally failed," thus verifying the old document found by Dr. Barton which he styled "Herndon's Unpublished Reason," to which we have already called the attention of the reader. And this daughter she calls "Sarah." The "only child" of Thomas and Nancy was first called "Nancy" after her own mother, but this girl's name was changed to "Sarah," after Tom married the widow, Sarah Bush Johnson (Lamon's *History*, p. 13). This story verifies the evidence that this boy was present at his mother's wedding and the various statements to the effect that he was not Tom Lincoln's son!

2. Their friends tried to fix the records to date back the marriage and "failed signally."

Now, why should she make this statement? Why should such a thing be thought of for one moment as changing the marriage record? What was the necessity for such procedure? What purpose could it serve in this case?

There is but one answer that any reasonable person can possibly give to these questions. And it is that this boy, called "Abraham Lincoln" was not Tom Lincoln's son, as charged by all the old people conversant with the situation in two different States.

And after the boy's mother died, the "friends" tried to fix the record to date back the marriage. Then this was done "after" his mother's death. His mother had nothing whatever to do with this deception. Now a number of surmises are possible right here. The "friends" could have made the attempt to make this boy "legitimate in the eyes of the law" and eliminate any scandal that might probably be encountered by the boy in the future. Or Tom Lincoln, himself, might have been the instigator of the scheme to get five years more service from this boy who was such "a good hand to work"!

It was stated by a good friend of Abraham Lincoln, with whom this young man often talked that "Old Tom was a hard task-master." And it may have been his plan to filch this boy out of a few of his best years! It certainly was not "to protect his mother" now. For she is where she doesn't need it.

And when one bores into his character and finds his "brutality" coupled with "a hard task-master" the conclusion that this step-father would not find it difficult to bring himself to just such an unholy undertaking, appears to be but reasonable.

It appears that Lincoln had more sense than old Tom and all these "friends" who tried to fix the records to date back the marriage. Lincoln knew that would not work. For the old marriage record would "rise up in judgment against him." But in the heat of the political campaign, when some were making it very embarrassing for this poor mortal, he found himself in the peculiar predicament which at one time confronted the noted Senator Zebulon Vance of Western North Carolina, who at that time was in his first political race as a very young and inexperienced candidate for the legislature. And after his opponent, a man of mature years, had frequently referred to Vance as "a mere boy, without any experience whatever," Vance, in a very suave and apologetic manner said, "Ladies and Gentlemen, I am exceedingly sorry for the matter which my good friend complains of, but my father and mother gave me no chance to have it otherwise, but if you will just pardon this mistake I will try to do better next time"! And it is said they pardoned the boy's "mistake" by electing him.

This shrewd politician, as Lincoln was sometimes called, knew he could not "date back the marriage," but he could date forward his own birthday! And instead of making the record older, he, if they would pardon the mistake this time, would get to be a few years younger! And they pardoned his mistake and elected this man to the Presidency of the United States! (Barton, p. 115)

Hence, he was the wrongly-named President, his right name being, as he said to his friend Davis, "Abraham Enloe."

CHAPTER TWENTY-EIGHT

☆ ☆ ☆ ☆

Lincoln's Letters and Nancy Hanks' Oven-Lid

Attorney J. Scroop Styles, a prominent citizen of Asheville, North Carolina, has contributed some very interesting data after I had thought I was through with this work. Mr. Styles is closely related to President Lincoln, and this material was handed over to him by his ancestors. His own mother being a granddaughter of Scroop Enloe, half brother of Lincoln. And on his father's side, this lawyer traces his ancestry back to Ezra Styles the founder and first president of Yale University. This record is fully documented.

Mr. Styles, in addition to verifying all of the traditional stories about the girl Nancy Hanks as an inmate of the home of his great-grandfather, Abraham Enloe, furnishes some strong additional testimony in this case.

Styles declares that while Lincoln was President of the United States, he often wrote to Robert Sellers, son-in-law of Scroop Enloe, then of Buncombe, North Carolina. Sellers was a young officer in the Union Army, and his old letters from the President were kept for a long time by Styles' own mother who was a daughter of Captain Sellers. Mr. Styles claims that he saw these letters, signed "A. Lincoln," when he was a small boy; but he has not seen them, he says, since his mother's house was burned in 1885, and he thinks the letters were then destroyed. It was known by all the family, says Styles, that a correspondence was carried on between Robert Sellers and President Lincoln.

Mr. Styles now has in his possession the old lid to the oven used by President Lincoln's mother. This girl stayed for several years in the home of Abraham Enloe, then of Buncombe County, N. C. and after her child was born she and the child were transported to Kentucky, where she soon married Thomas Lincoln. Some time after the Lincoln wedding, which was based upon an agreement with Abraham Enloe, father of the child, that he would pay Tom Lincoln five hundred dollars and a wagon and team for taking care of this illegitimate boy, the Lincoln family came to North Carolina to visit the Enloes and to collect on this marriage debt. At this time, as formerly noted in the Kennedy and the Melton testimony, Tom Lincoln was given a mare and mule and fifteen dollars in money (Kennedy). And at this time some things were given to Nancy, and among them was the old oven formerly used by Nancy in baking bread at the Enloes.

Then, after President Lincoln's tragic death, the lid to the old oven was found and secured by Mr. Styles' ancestors as a family treasure of the two families, the Enloes and the Lincolns.

The Old Indian Guide

Another corroborating story of interest is in regard to the first trip across the Great Smokey Mountains by Abraham Lincoln and his mother, Nancy Hanks, before she had ever seen Thomas Lincoln.

It is claimed that the dove of peace had flown away from the home of the well-to-do family of Enloes of Ocona Lufta, and it refused to return with an olive leaf so long as Nancy Hanks remained in North Carolina. This "Hagar" of mystery must leave the State; she must go far away to a strange country, before the white dove would return to that beautiful mountain-hugged home.

Taking Little Abraham to Kentucky

John Thompson, Enloe's son-in-law, takes the cast out girl and her child, the future President of the United States, to his own home, and President Lincoln rewards this kindness by appointing Mr. Thompson's son to an important position at the head of Disbursements for the Cherokee Indians in 1861.

the State; she must go far away to a strange country, before the white dove would return to that beautiful mountain-hugged home.

Mr. Enloe, being a "superior man" in many ways, was ready to do anything in his power to make amends satisfactory to Mrs. Enloe for the sake of the good family name and influence, but at the same time he feels that he is also morally bound to look after the interest of his "Hagar" and her boy named "Abraham" for him.

And the most feasible plan seemed to be to send the girl and child to the State of Kentucky to be cared for in the home of Mrs. Nancy Thompson, daughter of Enloe.

Of course this trip involved the difficulty of crossing the Great Smokey Mountains, which then were not free from danger, for not only "wild Indians" but savage and dangerous beasts roamed the dense forests of this uninhabited section of the country at this time.

However, there was an Indian trail across this country and an old Indian carried the mail over this mountain for a long time. His name was Triola Jessan; and Mr. Styles thinks that this mail carrier who worked in the service of the government for a half century, passing the Enloe home, was the son of the old Indian guide who piloted Nancy Hanks and the Thompsons over the big mountains into Tennessee on their way to Kentucky.

The old Indian, who was sometimes called "chief," lived to be 115 years old; and always wore a striped shawl over his shoulders, and a feathered head-gear appropriate to his caste and standing.

"This Indian often spoke of having served as guide for Nancy Hanks and the little party over the Smokey Mountains into Kentucky," says Mr. Styles; and that he always insisted that the girl called "Nancy Hanks" carried along with her on this trip a little "papoose."

The Indian said, "Nancy rode a spotted pony which he led over all the very rough spots on the trail while the girl held the baby (papoose) in her arms."

NOTE – It will be remembered that Dr. Barton, Lincoln Paternity historian, says he visited Asheville, N.C, and met Attorney Styles, and had a talk with him about Lincoln, but Styles claims he never met Barton at any time, unless Barton was working incognito.

CHAPTER TWENTY-NINE

☆ ☆ ☆ ☆

Summation of the Evidence

1. The overwhelming and unimpeachable evidence submitted by the Hon. James H. Cathey in his book *Truth Is Stranger Than Fiction* from which we have quoted in the first part of this book locates "Nancy Hanks" in North Carolina.

a) This was a "child of mystery," having been brought to North Carolina from Amelia County, Virginia, in the latter part of the 18th century in company with Hankses and Tanners, Michael Tanner being her father and Lucy Hanks being her mother, according to an old manuscript recently found in Rutherford County, North Carolina.

b) Lucy Hanks and this child "Nancy" made their home for some time with Lucy's brother, Richard, popularly known as "Dick" Hanks, who lived in a little log cabin on the Catawba River near the present town of Belmont, where a monument marks the early home of "Lincoln's mother."

c) When Nancy was a small child her mother Lucy went to Kentucky, probably in company with a number of emigrants including the Mitchels, Berrys, Thompsons, Lincolns and Hankses, leaving their early settlement on the Catawba River in North Carolina. And some time after her mother left this girl was placed in the home of Abraham Enloe, a "wealthy citizen of Rutherford County."

d) Two old documents written by members of the Tanner family reveal the "secret" in regard to this girl's true ancestry, her paternal ancestor being Michael Tanner "of the best blood of Virginia," pure German stock.

e) After the Enloes moved to the mountains, taking the girl "Nancy Hanks," as she was always called, along with the large family, she was driven from the Enloe home by Mrs. Enloe as a prospective "Hagar."

f) Her son was born on Puzzle Creek in Rutherford County, in the old home vacated by the Enloes when they left Rutherford County.

g) From here, in about 1804 or 1805, Abraham Enloe sent this girl to Kentucky where she and her boy named "Abraham," for Enloe his father, made their home for some time with the Thompsons, son-in-law and daughter of Enloe.

h) This girl soon married Thomas Lincoln in 1806, upon agreement with Abraham Enloe, father of the boy "that he would pay Thomas Lincoln a wagon and team and $500.00."

i) A savage fight occurred between Enloe and Thomas Lincoln, induced because of "brutal treatment" of little Abraham and his mother by Lincoln.

j) The belligerents made friends and the Lincolns visited the Enloe family in North Carolina and, upon this occasion collected "a mare and a mule and $15.00" on the amount due Lincoln.

Kentucky Stories Corroborate

The entire chain of Kentucky tradition tends to verify the above North Carolina stories.

a) Historians have pictured a "compound" or conglomerate "Nancy Hanks" without any child as the girl who married Thomas Lincoln. But she was too old, and she had the wrong mother and the wrong father, and was a blond instead of a brunette; Abraham Lincoln did not recognize her, and Thomas Lincoln never saw her.

b) Kentuckians claim that the girl who married Thomas Lincoln had a boy named Abraham when she was married to Lincoln, and this was reported as having been told by the minister who performed the marriage ceremony, and this was sworn to by Chief Justice Peters of the Kentucky Supreme Court, stating that "all the lawyers in the State of Kentucky believed this report."

c) This was verified by Judge Gilmore, who states that he knew the boy before his mother was married to Lincoln; they attended the same school and knew each other well.

d) It is further verified by Col. Davis, Attorney of St. Louis, Mo., who was well acquainted with the Lincoln family, and had appeared with Abraham Lincoln in cases before the Supreme Court of Illinois. And Col. Davis stated that he was well acquainted with the Lincoln family; that he knew Lincoln's mother before she was married, and that she then had a boy she called Abraham; and that it was the general understanding among the people that the man whom Nancy Hanks married was not the father of this boy, but that his father's name was "Abraham Enloe of North Carolina."

e) A similar statement to the above by Col. Davis was also published in a Tennessee paper in 1861, carrying a lengthy article, while Abraham Lincoln was President. And Judge Peters of Kentucky published the same in his paper at Mount Sterling, Kentucky; and an Illinois newspaper, during the Lincoln-Douglas campaign, asked the question, "Who is this man Lincoln?," and the answer was, "We don't know; all we know is that he is a son of 'Nancy Hanks.'" And Lincoln never replied to any of these queries. Such questions greatly embarrassed him.

f) Lincoln suffered the loss of many votes in Kentucky on account of the public reports that he was of "illegitimate" origin.

g) His friends got together and tried to "Ax the date" of the Lincoln wedding to include this "Abraham" as a legitimate heir of Thomas Lincoln, and signally failed.

h) A Kentucky story reported that an "Abraham Enloe got

mixed up with the hired girl and hired Tom Lincoln to marry her" (Barton, pp. 186, 187).

i) Austin Gallaher, school mate and an early friend of Abraham Lincoln, claims that he saved Lincoln's life from drowning in Knob Creek in 1812 and that they had been in school together the year before this June in which this happened. If he were born in 1809, he would have been too young, being just a little over three years old. And at this time "young Lincoln was a hunter and rover of the woods, eight years old" (Miss Tarbell; Nicolay and Hay, Vol. I, p. 27).

j) All of Lincoln's childhood history in Kentucky verifies the story by Austin Gallaher as to chronological accuracy and is out of harmony with the popular date of Lincoln's birth.

k) Kentucky people knew about the Lincoln-Enloe fight, and wrote it up in *Bledsoe's Magazine*, from which it went into the two earliest "Histories of Abraham Lincoln" (Lamon; Herndon).

l) It was reported in Kentucky that Nancy, Tom's wife, "died of heart trouble, from slander about her and old Abe Enloe, called Inloe, while her Abe was still little" (Graham affidavit).

m) Lincoln answered none of the many letters which he received during the campaigns, in regard to his illegitimacy (Herndon).

n) Lincoln agreed with Judge Helms that he (Lincoln) ate brown sugar at the store in Elizabethtown soon after Tom and Nancy were married but this was two years before the date 1809, popularly given as Lincoln's birthday; and Haycraft, historian, corroborates this by saying he knew the Lincolns there and often saw the little boy with his mother.

o) The historians are not able to find where Tom got the money to buy a farm, paying a substantial sum in cash.

p) Lincoln stated that he was not related to the noted Benjamin Lincoln, and that he did not know who was his grandfather.

q) Lincoln stated, confidentially, that his right name was Enloe, but that he had always gone by the name of his step-father.

Identification of the N.C. Girl as Lincoln's Mother

1. When the "scintillating" little blond is discarded it will give a place for the "Nancy Hanks" of North Carolina to fill the vacancy.

a) Abraham Lincoln stated to Herndon that his mother was the illegitimate daughter of Lucy Hanks and a well-bred Virginia farmer or planter of the best blood of Virginia. This one statement by this high authority discredits the "Hitchcock Nancy" of popular history as a girl too old by two years and who was not the "illegitimate daughter of Lucy Hanks and a well bred Virginia planter of the best blood of Virginia."

b) Lincoln must have a mother, and historians have not furnished any substitute for the blond, rejected by Abraham Lincoln, and the "Hagar" from the mountains of Western North Carolina with the little "Abe" is the only one to fit into this vacancy. She is the right age, since she is not yet 21, and it therefore was necessary for her to have someone sign her marriage bond; and her mother was "Lucy Hanks" who was never married till she went to Kentucky and married Henry Sparrow. And she (Nancy) was the illegitimate daughter of Michael Tanner, planter, "of the best blood of Virginia," according to secret and private records kept in the Tanner family. The Tanners were a German family who came to Virginia directly from Germany in the 18th century.

c) With the acceptance of the North Carolina Nancy, with her little Abraham, all the wrinkles are ironed out of the conflicting Kentucky stories. And the Enloes of North Carolina have a personal interest in the girl who married Thomas Lincoln. Enloe pays Lincoln to marry the girl with the little boy, and Enloe fights Tom for brutally whipping little Abe and Nancy. These Kentucky stories were founded upon facts, but what puzzled the historians was that they were unable to find the Abraham Enloe in Kentucky who had the fight with Tom Lincoln, and who was the father of this boy.

d) The startling testimony of Mrs. Manon, the daughter of John Hanks, residing in California a few years ago, is overwhelming proof of our contention. Mrs. Manon states that she knew all the Lincoln family and relatives, and that "Thomas and Nancy had one child, 'Sarah,' and their friends after Nancy's death tried to fix the records to date back the marriage, and failed signally" (Barton, p. 115).

With the accumulated circumstantial, corroborative and direct evidence herein offered, the case is substantially made out, proving that the North Carolina "Nancy Hanks" from Amelia County, Virginia, daughter of Michael Tanner and Lucy Hanks, reared in the home of Abraham Enloe and sent to Kentucky with a baby named "Abraham," the woman who married Tom Lincoln and who was whipped by Tom and whose husband was forced to fight Enloe for his brutality to this woman and child, and whose husband afterwards visited this Enloe to collect a mare and mule and money on a former agreement, was the mother of Abraham Lincoln.

CHAPTER THIRTY

☆ ☆ ☆ ☆

A Biographical Sketch of Abraham Enloe

The following is a contribution by Hon. James H. Cathey:

Abraham Enloe, the traditional father of Abraham Lincoln, was the son of Gilbert Enloe, and was born in York District, South Carolina. The first of his American forebears came from Scotland about the middle of the seventeenth century. They landed first in Maryland, where they settled. They were school teachers.

Abraham's father, being a man of more than ordinary mental gifts, the son received the rudiments of a good education. On coming of age he stepped from under his father's roof into the world to seek his fortune.

As a boy, he was obedient and industrious and had made the most of his father's splendid tuition. He was, therefore, well equipped for one of his day for the struggle for life. He was of an excellent temper and judgment while yet a youth. He illustrated these in his choice of a country and clime in which to exercise his vigorous young faculties, as well as in the selection of a wife to share with him in their fruitions.

He sought a home first in Rutherford County, North Carolina, where he became acquainted with a Miss Egerton, a young

Trees Used As Brakes

They often encountered very steep places in the trail, and to avoid a stampede or runaway down these places, they tied small trees to the rear ends of the wagons.

young lady of intellect and culture, and a member of one of the best families in that section of the State. Their acquaintance at once ripened into genuine affection, and they were married and settled down to farming. While a citizen of Rutherford County, he established a reputation for uprightness of character which is still recalled with pride by his neighbors and which followed him to his new home and throughout his life.

About the year 1803 to 1805, while early settlers were "staking their claims" further west, this man emigrated from Rutherford County and stopped on the Ocona Lufta, at the base of the Great Smokey Mountains in Buncombe County, now Jackson.

In the settlement of his new home he encountered the usual difficulties of the pioneer. His granddaughter, a Mrs. Floyd, a bright and entertaining woman, said she remembered hearing her grandfather recount his experiences in coming to this place, and while trying to establish himself on Ocona Lufta. The journey from Rutherfordton over great mountains and across dangerous streams was fraught with labor and peril. They were often compelled to improvise causeways for creeks and rivers, or to construct breastworks and dig wider the ways of the more primitive adventurers along the almost perpendicular mountain sides. When they had thus reached the summit of high mountains, so steep was the descent that they were obliged to tie good bits of trees to the rear ends of their wagons to prevent stampeding the teams. It was not infrequent that, because of the absence of any way save a deer or Indian trail, they packed their effects piecemeal on their backs over formidable mountains.

He was, however, fortunate in the choice of a stopping place. The Ocona Lufta is in the center of the highlands of the South, midway between the Hiwassee, Tennessee, and Nantahala on the one side, and the Tuckuseegih, French Broad and Swannanoa on the other.

It was a land to make the heart of the strong man grow stronger. The soil was rich. The trees were original. The air was pure. The water was crystal. And the forests were alive with a very great variety of birds and animals. It was a land whose star was not wormwood, but bright hope.

The only neighbors that were near to them after he had built his house were three families, who had accompanied him from Rutherford, and the Cherokee Indians, in the heart of whose region he was.

There were other White families, living within a distance of from twelve to fifty miles. A settlement in those days embraced a circuit of from twelve to fifty miles, and was made up of as many families. It was such a settlement as this of which Abraham Enloe was the central figure and benefactor. In obedience to an ancient custom of mankind, each society or neighborhood, however small, must have its leading spirit and par-excellent advisor. Particularly must this needs be the practice of a community where the frequent hostilities of the aborigines, whose grievance is by no means imaginary, must be met. The common interest must be healthful and steadfast.

Abraham Enloe built his house in a fertile valley overlooking the Ocona Lufta, whose banks in summer are a continuous string of bouquets: Rhododendron, ivy (Kalmia), and honeysuckle, to this day. It is an incident worthy of note here, that this house is still standing, but slightly remodeled [now torn down]; and has been in four Counties without being removed from its original foundation. It is a typical pioneer abode. One large log house with doors in either side directly opposite each other, and a chimney at one end built of natural boulders, with a remarkably wide fireplace.

A sure reminder of the brotherhood of the frontier community was the uniform nature of the settlers' habitations. The style and value of the houses were as near the same as primitive ingenuity and limited resources could make them. No envy arose in the breast of the pioneer because of striking contrasts. The cabin did not droop and shiver in the shadow of the palace. Every man that crossed the settler's threshold crossed it like a knight.

Notwithstanding Abraham Enloe was generally absorbed in the more serious concerns of life, he found time for the then profitable diversion of hunting. The long-barreled flintlock was ever "picked" and "primed" for emergency use. The haunts of the deer, bear, and wild turkey were just outside his enclosure, and many are the thrilling stories of delightful sport in which he was always joined by some of his neighbors. On his broad door step and on the clean yard sat or slumbered long-eared deerhounds, watchful curs or surly mastiffs. Each of these bided patiently his call to dinner or duty, and all were indispensable in their respective spheres as followers of the chase, guards of the plantation and protectors of the home.

Returning once from the home of the Hon. Felix Walker, whose place was west of the settlement a distance of fifty miles, Mrs. Enloe was amused to see her husband alight from his horse, across whose withers was a white bag either end of which was strangely animate. Her wonder was turned to ridicule when she learned that the queer sack contained four fine deerhound puppies, the gift of the clever Congressman. The pioneer would almost as readily have given up his rifle as his dogs. The keen solicitude which the settlers felt and manifested for these noble animals and the tender attachment which they in turn made known to their masters in their heroic encounters with savage beasts and more savage men, appeal to our highest sensibilities. Their estimation was shared by men, women, and children, and this no doubt helped to tie the Gordian knot of good-neighborhood.

Abraham Enloe owned the best and at first the only horses in the neighborhood. He greatly valued these splendid animals, as well for their beauty as their utility, and allowed nothing to go undone that would make them appear to the best advantage.

He was by profession a farmer, and early set a progressive pace for his neighbors in his chosen calling. He also possessed the only forge and blacksmith tools in the settlement, with which he kept in repair the farming implements of himself and neighbors.

There were no stores, and the nearest markets to which the settlements had access were at Augusta, Ga., and Charleston, S.C. To these places, distant hundreds of miles over the roughest of country and rudest of way, the settler hauled his produce or drove his live stock, which he eagerly exchanged for the necessities of civilized life.

Abraham Enloe possessed the only wagon in the settlement, and this served to transport at one trip the salt, powder and domestic consumed for a twelvemonth. Learning on a certain occasion that the settlement's meager supply of salt was exhausted, he harnessed his team, collected a few choice steers from his herd and started for Augusta, Ga., where a fresh supply of this indispensable was procured, not only for himself but for each of his neighbors.

He was a Justice of the Peace, an office of no little dignity in primitive times, and he was implicitly turned to as the final arbiter in adjusting differences between his neighbors. He was the trusted advisor of the politicians, great and small, of his party, with whom he came in contact. The relations existing between himself and the Hon. Felix Walker, the first member of Congress from the Buncombe district, were the most cordial and intimate.

It was this same Felix Walker, a discreet leader of frontiersmen, who while delivering himself of legislative responsibility in a speech of some length in the House of Representatives, and observing what he construed to be an expression of weariness on the face of the Speaker and members, raised himself to his full height and assured them that he was aware of the fact that he had spoken at some length; that what he was saying might not interest them but that it was his firm resolve to continue until he had done, and then with reassured emphasis, he said, "Mr. Speaker, I wish the gentlemen of this House to understand that I am speaking for Buncombe."

The house of Abraham Enloe was headquarters for the gospel. The pioneer preacher, no matter his creed, found there a warm welcome and partook of his hospitalities without the semblance of grudge.

Public worship was one of the strongest bonds of these early communities. At a period too early for the log church, they came for many miles to the house of some prominent settler to an annual or semiannual appointment of such men as brave old Cartwright or the brilliant Bascum. To them worship was not a mere diversion. It was a solemn responsibility and means of power that must be seriously regarded. Earnestness fitted them like a garment. They came to the place appointed for worship, if it was the mild season, in their shirt sleeves with their rifles on their shoulders. They were the synonym of simplicity, and every declaration based upon a straight interpretation of the Bible they accepted eagerly and without question.

With them there were few base coins; most were ringing, bright gold. From them have sprung like wheat from virgin soil, the harvest of heroic men, whose mission it is to meet and turn aside the wild, babbling stream of innovation which now and then threatens to mingle its noxious floods with the old abiding river of human progress.

Abraham Enloe's house was often converted into a settlement sanctuary. It was little more than a half dozen miles from his house to the Capitol of the Cherokees. His policy toward these children of the forest was benevolence – the true neighbor, while White men of other settlements often provoked a "hurrying to and fro" upon the war-path, Abraham Enloe and his dusky neighbors snugly reclined in the bosom of peace.

Establishing a Friendship With the Cherokee Indians

Abraham Enloe was a man of great conservation and judgment. There was no rashness in his nature.

He, therefore, sought among the first things after settling in Western North Carolina, to establish a permanent friendship between himself and the Chief and most influential men of the Cherokees. He ever enjoyed the respect and confidence of the band, and his relations with the two chiefs, Yonaguskah and Sawinookih, were the most intimate and pleasant.

It was indeed fortunate for Abraham Enloe and his neighbors that they were contemporaries of such dynasties as those of Yonaguskah and Sawinookih. These chiefs were both men of great natural ability, especially Yonaguskah. He was pronounced by a competent judge, who knew both well, the intellectual peer of John C. Calhoun.

The following story, as told by Col. W. H. Thomas who was an eye witness, will serve to illustrate the superstitious wisdom of this old chief. The Cherokees, like most men of their race who come too near the blessed influence of Caucasian civilization, became addicted to strong drink. Yonaguskah, though himself an occasional victim of its subtle embraces, determined upon the prohibition of strong drink among his entire band. Suddenly he fell into a stupor. So deep and mysterious were his slumbers that the whole town heard of it. They came flocking to his side and looked long and very sadly upon him and decided that he was dead. In agony they waited for the return of their venerable chief to his senses and his wondrous walks and ways. But no sign of life appeared, and over a thousand of his faithful children determined, in deep sorrow, to celebrate their ancient and impressive rite of funeral and sepulchre. Forming in a single file, they danced around the prostrate Chief mumbling their weird death-chant.

Suddenly, in the midst of the solemn performance, Yonaguskah arose and standing in their midst with the inspiration of a prophet and majesty of a king, told them that he had been transplanted to the "happy hunting grounds," and that while there he had communed with the Great Spirit relative to their happiness. He said he was impressed that intemperance would be the means of their extermination, and advised them to turn their back on the "fire water" of the White man. He said he had served them over forty years without asking for a cent of pay, and the only thing he exacted was their obedience. With profound feeling he bemoaned his own and his people's mistake, and concluded by directing Col. Thomas to act as clerk and write the following:

"The undersigned Cherokees, belonging to the town of Qualla, agree to abandon the use of spirituous liquors."

Gravely stepping forward the old Chief signed first and was then followed by the whole town. For many years this pledge was kept inviolate, and at last, when some yielded to the influence of the Whites and were led to break it, Yonaguskah established the "whipping post" and enforced his simple pledge with the rigor of an English statute in the reign of Henry the Eighth.

Sawinookih was a man of great native wit. In one of his visits as Chief to Washington, he imbibed a little too prodigally of "fire water," and wandering around in the bewildering glare of lights and city pageant (for it was in the night), he became "lost" and leaned up against the corner of a building for the night. In the midst of his dozings a passer-by accosted him with "Hello, Indian, aren't you lost?" to which he instantly replied "No! Injun not lost; hotel lost!"

Abraham Enloe was a large stock dealer for his day. It was his custom to drive annually cattle, horses and mules to Southern markets, and by this and the acquisition of large tracts of land and the slave trade, he accumulated considerable means and established a reputation at home and in the marts of the South for prominent judgment and far-reaching business acumen.

He trafficked in Negroes all the way from Western North Carolina to Florida. From the latter, on one occasion, he brought home twenty. He was kind to his slaves. A practical example of his benevolence toward them was shown in his habitual custom of reading and expounding to them the Holy Scriptures each Sabbath.

He is described by those who were intimate with him to have been possessed of a fund of anecdote. He was also rich in practical humor. When he would take the Sunday morning's "tanseydram" of which the pioneer was famously though temperately fond, he would call up his little Negroes and, causing them to stick out their big underlips, he would, with much dignity, pour a teaspoonful on each protruded lip to the infinite amusement of the family and the exquisite pleasure of the little ebonites themselves.

In his private life, Abraham Enloe was cordially esteemed by his neighbors; in his family he ruled with patience and firmness. He was the father of nine sons and seven daughters. The sons all lived to man's estate, the only surviving one of whom says that each of the nine remained under parental control until he was of age, and not one was ever known to rebel against his father.

In personal appearance he is described by the family and those who knew him as having been a very large man, perhaps more, not less, than six feet high. Not corpulent, but muscular and very sinewy. His head was large and fine. Forehead and nose and mouth were prominent. His hair was stiff and black. His complexion was inclined to be tawny. Unfortunately, there is no likeness of him in existence. Men of his time didn't set much by pictures, and artists were scarce in the land.

He was undoubtedly a man of extraordinary mind. It is the universal consensus that he was the strongest character in his section, as plain, practical, unaspiring citizen. As heretofore intimated, his judgment was cheerfully deferred to or eagerly sought by his fellow citizens on subjects and occasions of moment.

He was simple, honest, brave; an ardent friend of truth. He hesitated not to go on toilsome errands of mercy for his bereft neighbors. He asked nothing in return but the answer of a good conscience. He was the best type of the civilian; plain, honest, unselfish. He had faults, but they were not such as rise from a mean heart plunged in moral turpitude, but those to which the flesh is easily heir. He was not a saint, but what is better here below, a nature's nobleman (Hon. James H. Cathey, in his book *Truth Stranger Than Fiction*, pp. 122-140).

* * * *

The foregoing tribute to Abraham Enloe, the real father of Abraham Lincoln, by the Hon. Mr. Cathey brings out some wonderfully striking similarities in the peculiar characteristics of Enloe which appear in his son by Nancy Hanks. No one can read this biographical sketch and not be moved by the fact that Abraham Lincoln was as near a perfect picture of his father, Abraham Enloe, as a son could possibly be of his father!

And this fact was published in the old county newspaper at Rutherfordton shortly after the war upon the appearance of President Lincoln's picture in the papers. Colonel Albert Logan, of Rutherfordton, North Carolina, stated that the picture of Lincoln could be passed upon anybody who knew Abraham Enloe for his picture! That the resemblance was perfect and the mental ability and traits of these men were very similar.

APPENDIX

A Tribute to Abraham Lincoln
By Hon. James H. Cathey

Born no one knoweth where or when, he arose out of the bramble of obscurity. Whether he first saw the light in the woods, on the roadside, or in a dingy hovel, it matters not. He was nature's child, and nature nursed him. With her blessing she dropped him on the world and bade him live. He was first a helpless infant, then a little toddling child, then a boy, but unlike other boys he was awkward and gawky; his legs and arms were longer, his hands and feet were larger than those of other boys. He was more diffident and silent than any other boy.

At seven he went to school and learned to read; at ten he learned to write. He was serious and thoughtful; not too much energetic in body, but stint and duty urged him on, and he wielded the ax at the age of eight (?) and did the milling.

Reaching youth, he remained in school, procured books and applied himself diligently. He stepped at once to the head of his class, and when a pretty schoolmate in spelling a word hesitated, to know whether to say i or y, he pointed to his eye; she spelled it and the teacher, unobservant, passed on.

He loved books. He eagerly devoured all there was in the

secular home library of three books and turned his eye in search of others. He made himself familiar with the best literature of the neighborhood for miles around. His nightly companions were such sacred, old standards as the Bible, *Aesop's Fables, Robinson Crusoe,* Bunyan's *Pilgrim's Progress,* and Weem's *Life of Washington.* He borrowed the latter from a penurious neighbor, placed it in the crack between the logs of the cabin overnight; there came a rain which wet the book and the boy carried it to the owner to assess the damage; the owner said twenty-five cents, and the young Lincoln pulled fodder three days to satisfy him.

At the age of sixteen he wrote a dissertation on temperance and essayed poetry.

He grew to be a man, and he wanted, instead of his buckskin, a pair of brown jeans panteloons, and he split for an old lady four hundred rails for every yard of cloth it took to make them. He read, he wrote, he spoke, he lectured, he farmed, he split rails, he pitched quoits, he joked, he wrestled, and sometimes he fought a fisticuff.

He became a surveyor; he studied the statutes of Indiana and practiced stump-speaking in the field to the hands.

He assisted in the management of a ferry across the Ohio River at thirty-seven and one-half cents a day; was noted as being the strongest man in the settlement, and was equally famous for writing papers on the science of government. He acted as bow-hand on a boat in a voyage to New Orleans at a salary of eight dollars a month, and made three thousand rails for one man, walking three miles each day to his work.

He was a religious free-thinker and an adept at anecdote. He became a loaf in New Salem, Illinois, and then clerk to an election board. He was a miller and then a clerk in a store.

He was a merchant, and studied English. He was a hero in an interesting love affair, and came near fighting a duel.

He was Captain of a Company in the Black Hawk war, and read law meanwhile.

He was elected to the legislature, and later was admitted to the bar. He was one of the foremost lawyers in the State of Illinois, and the rival of Stephen A. Douglas for the heart of a charming blue-blooded girl; he vanquished the Judge and obtained her hand in marriage.

He was a frequent contributor to the political journals, and attained a local prominence as a campaigner and manager.

He was elected to Congress and never opened his mouth except to vote.

He stepped upon the hustings against the "Little Giant," and attracted the notice of the entire country by his resource and facility at repartee.

He was an orator of rare felicity, and a statesman of extraordinary sagacity.

He endeavored to lecture on the "History and Progress of Inventions," and ignominiously failed. He was invited to Cooper Institute to speak. He accepted the invitation, spoke on "The Political Issues of the Day," and paved his way to the Presidency.

He was nominated for the Chief Ministry of the nation over the trained diplomat and statesman, William H. Seward, and was elected over three other candidates, one of whom was his old-time rival, Stephen A. Douglas. He occupied the executive chair through the most horrible war of all history; was elected to a second term during the progress of that war, and just as he was adjusting his great faculties to lead the nation into a glorious peace, he was stricken by the red hand of an assassin.

History affords no parallel to Abraham Lincoln. In the classification of the world's heroes he stands alone.

In the commingling and jargon of the common mass he stood the tall representative of a new type.

His ways were of his own making. With his face set straight forward, his long arms swinging heavily, he strode so mightily that not only his own countrymen did list, but his footfall echoed around the world. Now, he rose up, up, until he reached the heights, and then he grappled with the earth and made those who touched him feel that they had touched a kindred clay.

His was a many-sided nature – an antithetical life – and his career was as mixed and varying as his nature was unique and odd.

Abraham Lincoln will never be understood. He may be appreciated, but it will require an exhaustive study of his character to enable one to do so.

He possessed an intellect deep and keen. He could see as far into profound and difficult questions as any man contemporaneous with him or, doubtless, who has followed him.

He had a will, a will that was volatile or immovable at the command of his soul. On subjects of grave import his will, becoming fixed, was not to be swerved a hair's breadth; on questions indifferent and small, his volition was the obedient child of policy and expediency. His mind was no less subtle than logical in its operation. His judgment was as clear and unerring as mortal's usually is.

His heart was large, good and tender as that of a child. It was responsive in the highest and best degree. No one in distress ever appealed to him in vain. A great, picturesque rock in a dry and thirsty land, the weary traveler rested in its shade.

As Abraham Lincoln emerged from the wilderness into civilization's highway men looked on him and were amazed. Whence did he come and whither was he bound? Lincoln beheld their wonder. He read their very thoughts, and herein was his mystery. In his intuitive knowledge of men, he towered like the giant he was far above his fellows.

He early, how early we know not, became conscious that he was a man, and learned to associate with men as such. He did not have to come down on the common human level – he walked up and down between the clods from which he sprang and to which he sadly sank. In matters of conscience the angel of his better nature was his guide. He was not a Christian in the popular sense, traceable no doubt to the bereavement of his mother. He had no faith in the orthodox sense; his faith was reason, the logic of cause and effect. His reliance was firm in God and immortality; his religion materialized in deeds whose end was to make humanity better. He was not a dreamer, but an intense practicalist. Of this his life bore abundant evidence. By this it is not meant that he could not scheme or plan upon the largest scale. This he did. But, like Alexander and Napoleon, he executed as rapidly as he planned. His genius was the most fertile and versatile. No exigency arose to confound his faculties and baffle his resource. In the fiercest administrative storm he stood on the topmost billow like a Norseman of old, unterrified. In the midst of these perplexities, when his associates were all dismayed, he related a humorous anecdote about some good farmer in Illinois, and transformed the scene of distraction into hilarious uproar.

He believed in the right and ability of mankind to govern themselves. He did not hesitate to avow at the same time, "that all of the people might do wrong part of the time."

He was a man of the most profound principle. He was preeminently a man of policy. Principle was an end, policy was the means.

He was courageous physically, intellectually, morally. He shrank not from physical contests the most taxing.

He was eager to cross mental swords with the most brilliant.

He antagonized old, sacred beliefs in politics and religion with weird audacity, and his antagonist always bore away marks of the engagement.

He always weighed well his words and calculated cooly his acts; their effect was reckoned before they left him.

He was ambitious. He was aspiring. He was restless. He sighted his object, and then thought and planned and strove to reach it.

He was certain of his powers, and he wielded them with a careful hand. There was no slumbering talent with him; no rust or ashes with the broken pottery of neglect in the paths he frequented.

Like some precious tree that regales the passer-by with its delightful perfume, he imparted a sweet influence to all who passed through the atmosphere of his being.

While others studied books, Lincoln studied men. Here was another real secret of his life. From his plain Western home he looked abroad and surveyed the field. With a wise and cunning eye he looked at the East with her Phillips and her Sumner; the North with her Seward and her Cameron; the Middle West and West with their Corwin and Chase – men of his own political party; men of vaulting ambition and commanding talent – and wondered how he might pass through them into the White House of the nation.

He outwitted, outthought, outdid a rival, no matter how great, and then looking back at the hill of success, he bound up that rival's broken hope by an unseen stratagem. Thus he made secretaries, generals and justices of the Supreme Court.

He was a superb tactician. He laid his plans with the utmost precision, and these rarely miscarried.

When he formulated a purpose, he often consulted the minds of others, but in the end he preferred his own judgment and upon it risked the issue.

He was frank and open in his general intercourse, but there was a well-known line in his character where publicity stopped and privacy began. This discipline made his insight into the public men with whom he dealt approximate omniscience. He knew their strong points, their virtues, and he knew their faults and foibles. He read their whims and caprices as one would read a book.

He unbosomed himself to none; he risked many and trusted few. He collided with men who in some particular field outshone him for a moment, but it was only for a moment; he had but to stand up and his simple personality overshadowed them. There was but one other person who possessed such simplicity and majesty of character in our country, and that was Robert E. Lee.

He knew the people, the plain folks, as he was pleased to style them, as no man has known them since the nation was born. He was of them. Through the white portals of the Capitol of the republic he looked into the lowly doors of millions of cabins each day of his four years of official incumbency. He saw the struggle and toil, the grief and tears; he felt them. As their faithful servant he remembered them and conducted their affairs with a view to their peace, prosperity and happiness. He knew their mode of thinking. He was conversant with their manner of speaking. He was familiar with their way of acting. He thought, spoke and acted as if he were in their presence. When he saluted them or took them by the hand, there was a meeting of friends. He was the prince of plain men, and they were his neighbors. He communicated with them in the simplest speech enlightened by homely illustration. With an endless supply of fable and anecdote he amused and instructed.

He loved and served the people, and the people loved and honored him. When it came to dealing with the people, he had no patience with the time-server. He was bold when he dealt with the people. He invited the most rigid scrutiny of his public acts. He promulgated his conviction or policy, defended it through every stage of its progress, and if it failed of its object he acknowledged his mistake and assumed the responsibility. He sounded the public necessity and sought to satisfy it fully.

Trickery and simulation were foreign to him. If he thought he was being imposed upon, woe be to the imposter. If it was without his power to aid a friend, he frankly told him so. He was very charitable in the high catholic sense. He had a tender fellow-feeling for mankind. He knew the many weaknesses to which the flesh is heir. He was sure to see the suffering heart, and no one ever touched it more often to soothe.

He frequently withdrew from the multitude and communed with himself. He came forth stronger when he had encountered a difficulty. He left the dross in the fire; sorrow and tribulation were his earthly lot. "Myrrh and aloes and ivory palaces" turned not his head; he was touched but not influenced by praise; he was often mortified but never unmanned by criticism. The ludicrous filled him with life; sorrow and suffering melted his big heart. He never fawned upon the public or an individual, and he was thought by some to be selfish and austere. He never meddled with the affairs of others, and he was accused of seeking personal aggrandizement.

In the practice of the law he was natural and urbane, and he was called a "monkey" and "clown." He was cautious and conservative in the exercise of his official functions, and he was suspicioned and criticized by the impetuous who should have been his warmest friends.

As president, he was not impervious to adverse political criticism or personal detraction, and he made fewer mistakes than any man who has yet filled that exalted station.

In private life he was natural, original to the point of eccentricity.

He was by nature a melancholy man; he drew it from his mother. The purple lineaments of this inward ghost shone from his pale and haggard face. At times this spirit well-nigh overcame him. But he asserted his mighty will. He courted the nymph of humor; he gathered stories full of mirth and of moral and told them to his company, and the wide prairie, the disordered law-office, or the executive chamber rang with jocund laughter. He was a patient husband, a lenient, loving father. He was no conventionalist; he cared less than nothing for fad or fashion; he was insensible to gossip and had no part or lot in the little strivings of small men. With him there were no petty likes and dislikes, nothing mean or groveling. He hated simpering flattery or growling churl with a mortal hatred. He was forgiving, sympathetic, kind; a broad-minded, great-hearted gentleman.

He was an American – the first American illustrating the existence of a new national type. He was the first popularly-acknowledged representative of the plebian cast; the first prince of American peasants, and lifting him upon their shoulders they proclaimed him the first yeoman of their freehold.

Of Southern origin, born in the South, he came up on a Western prairie. To Southern inheritance was added Western environment. To Southern warmth and generosity, springing from Southern sun and soil, was added the freedom of the Western plain and the rough habits of Western life. He was by nature and education the product of rural energy. The South and West were the home of this element. Of this element Lincoln was the untrammeled child. His parents never dreamed of Northern or Eastern sticklings, for ancient trans-Atlantic customs and laws. Such were his early surroundings, and so soon did he leave the South that he never had any prepossessions in favor of human slavery.

He was a simple though strong individual, and the oracle of his class, the masses, everywhere. The blessings of his virtuous mind and provident hand in due time began to fall upon all.

His influence no partisanship could destroy or faction avoid.

He was a patriot. He loved his country for his country's sake. He sought to cement the common interest and advance the common weal.

He was a steadfast believer in, and supporter of, the Constitution. He studied and construed it. He advocated a perpetual Union, and would not admit the right of any State to withdraw from it. He labored as no man ever has or ever will to preserve the Union unimpaired. This was the sole and only object of his chief magisterial life. He was opposed to the extension of human slavery into new territory, but "it was never his inclination or purpose to interfere with that institution in the States where it did exist." He deprecated the idea of freeing the colored race and turning them loose, clothed with equal rights, among the White people of the South. If he had lived, it never would have been done. He was the great central, controlling spirit on the Union side, and he waged the war on purely defensive grounds. The noble people of the North and East, though blood of our blood, did not realize the situation. Their splendid humanitarianism was too long-ranged. Not by striking the shackles from the colored race, for that was right, but by making him the equal of all of us whom they would not acknowledge the equal of a single man of them, they decreed we should wander in the wilderness of problem and uncertainty, not for forty years, but indefinitely.

Lincoln understood this, and his great heart went out in sympathy for the bleeding South. He knew that he was the son of her bosom and that her children were his brethren. He labored as long as there was a shadow of hope to avert the war. When its crimson tide began to flow, he proposed to buy the slaves and stop it.

Failing in this, he endeavored to colonize them beyond the

choler of unhappy memory and the antipathy of strange blood.

Persistent, firm and gentle in his memory of the South, he bore up against the pressure from the North to arm the black man against his former master. But when, at last, he saw that unless something was done his fondest dream would come to naught, he reluctantly gave way, and a portion of the slaves were made to lift their hands against us.

The stricken South lost this noble friend, her filial scion, when least she could afford it. Wilkes Booth might well have stayed the deadly hand, for if he had the South had journeyed round the valley through which she is passing.

But happily the time is now when the generous people of the North and East, who with the wisdom of prophecy picked Mr. Lincoln up at his opportunity and placed him where God intended, are seeing their mistake, and with the same candor and zeal which marked their strife, to bring about our problem, are essaying to help us solve it.

America has produced and will produce but one Lincoln! The world may now see but shall not soon understand this enigmatical man!

Reference: Hon. James H. Cathey, *Truth Is Stranger Than Fiction.*

www.ingramcontent.com/pod-product-compliance
Lightning Source LLC
Chambersburg PA
CBHW070557100426
42744CB00006B/308